THE ILLEGAL DIVERSION OF AIRCRAFT AND INTERNATIONAL LAW

THE ILLEGAL DIVERSION OF AIRCRAFT AND INTERNATIONAL LAW

by

Edward McWhinney

1975

A. W. Sijthoff - Leyden

BY THE SAME AUTHOR

As Author:
Judicial Review.
Föderalismus und Bundesverfassungsrecht.
Constitutionalism in Germany.
Comparative Federalism.
"Peaceful Coexistence" and Soviet-Western International Law.
Federal Constitution-Making for a Multi-National World.
International Law and World Revolution.
Conflit idéologique et Ordre public mondial.

As Editor:
Canadian Jurisprudence. The Civil Law and Common Law in Canada.
Law, Foreign Policy, and the East-West détente.
The Freedom of the Air (with M. A. Bradley).
New Frontiers in Space Law (with M. A. Bradley).
The International Law of Communications.
Aerial Piracy and International Law.
Federalism and Supreme Courts and the Integration of Legal Systems (with Pierre Pescatore an Raymond Baeyens).

ISBN 90 286 0155 4

Printed in the Netherlands.

TABLE OF CONTENTS

INTRODUCTION

AERIAL PIRACY AS AN EXERCISE IN INTERNATIONAL LEGAL PROBLEM-SOLVING

The within lectures were presented to the 50th Anniversary session of The Hague Academy of International Law in 1973, and delivered in the opening week of the session in the first week of July, 1973. They have since been published in the *Recueil des Cours de l'Académie de la Haye,* Volume I—1973, pages 261-372.

The subject of the illegal diversion of aircraft and of the development of effective means for its legal control is of intense interest today not merely to members of the "special legal community" of the air—the major airline companies (both governmental and private, commercial), the airline companies' air-crew and ground personnel, the airline passengers—but also to all those concerned with the broader problem of control of Terrorism of which, in its current international manifestations, the illegal diversion of aircraft has simply been one of the more striking and dramatic examples. All this has counselled the merits of publishing these lectures in separate, hard-cover, book form so that they can become more readily available to the general public outside the more specialised international law fraternity.

The illegal diversion of aircraft—or, in its more popular usage, aerial hijacking, and (somewhat less accurately) aerial piracy,—is, so far as it concerns international lawyers, really not one problem but a series of different and sometimes not always related problems. The approach to the definition of the problem-area indicates its basic polycentricity: for the problem-area encompasses the "political escape" hijackings that commenced with the Cold War era and have continued, rather more intermittently, up to the present, including the most recent religious refugee examples; the "lunatic fringe" hijackings which are, of course, sometimes accompanied by claims to a *bona fide* political motive on the part of their perpetrators who may, indeed, occasionally genuinely believe that they hold such a motive; the "hijacking for profit" (or "sky bandit") hijackings, a phenomenon of quite recent years where the prime motive has clearly been instant, large-scale financial gain; and, finally, the "international terrorist" (or "irregular combatancy") hijackings where, among a plethora of different motives, the dominant one is clearly to carry on or continue hitherto unresolved international conflicts by novel and unconventional means which, by their very nature, carry an unusually high degree of international publicity value.

The first main enquiry in the present lectures has been as to whether a complex, polycentric-type problem-situation has not been treated monolithically for conventional legal analysis and classification purposes simply because the often quite distinct and different problems or sub-problems involved within it have found their physical expression and outlet in the one particular act—namely the act of hijacking, which is sometimes purely symbolic in character, sometimes quite functional, and sometimes a mixture of both. On this view, this particular somewhat casual and fortuitous fact has tended to produce an essentially uniform or monolithic approach to all aspects of the problem-situation, that may have unnecessarily delayed the solution of individual aspects of the problem-situation while at the same time frustrating any over-all or comprehensive solution.

As a second main subject, the lectures examine the "special legal community"—to borrow Stammler's term—involved in the problem of aerial hijacking, in its various aspects. To be sure, in an increasingly interdependent World, all nation-states are concerned today, in some way or other, with aerial transportation; but the degree of national interest in aerial transportation obviously corresponds in measure to the degree of direct economic and political-strategic involvement, with the Big Powers, and the major airline countries too, clearly having, because of their substantial world-wide investments in aircraft and air routes, a far greater concern than other countries with ensuring the safety and regularity of aerial transportation as a whole. In terms of international organization, there are both general or multi-purpose organs like the United Nations General Assembly and Security Council, and also more specialized or limited-purpose international organizations like the International Civil Aviation Organization (ICAO). There are also international private (commercial) institutions like the International Air Transport Association (IATA), with the often highly intricate and subtle relationships between the IATA-developed economic infra-structure of cartel-style, inter-airline price-fixing agreements and special commercial arrangements, and the international air law superstructure as maintained or created through ICAO. Beyond that, there are the international private associations (pressure groups) like the International Federation of Airline Pilots' Associations (IFALPA); and finally the other, and too frequently overlooked participants in the international air transportation process, like the individual passengers. The conclusion emerging from this examination suggests that while all of these participants in the international law-making process do share a common interest in ensuring the safety and regularity of aerial transportation, they do not all necessarily give it the same weight or the same degree of priority in competition with other, competing values; nor do they necessarily agree on the choice of instruments (means) for best effectuating that interest, or on the degree of investment of social resources (including force) in those instruments. The lack of a basic identity of attitudes and expectations on the part of all participants in the international law-making process has certainly been one of the factors rendering difficult any really effective or timely community responses to the hijacking problem.

As a third main subject, the lectures venture upon an extended excursus on international legal problem-solving—its means and techniques—with particular regard to the control of hijacking. We begin with the treaty route—the multilateral treaty,—and include here an examination of the frequent gap between the treaty-signing and treaty-ratification, and an examination also of the relation between the number of parties to a treaty and the specificity (or lack of specificity) of that treaty; and then go on to attempt some appraisal of the multilateral treaty as a prime instrument for international problem-solving—its merits and its limitations—both in general, and also in relation to the specific problem of aerial hijacking. The main studies, here, focus upon the Tokyo Convention of 1963, The Hague Convention of 1970, and the Montreal Convention of 1971. We then examine the bilateral treaty-based approach, including, of course, the developing patterns of inter-locking or parallel systems of bilateral treaties in particular areas; informal bilateral accords (being less than treaties); international private action—through IATA first of all, and then self help-style boycott action through IFALPA and other organizations. We also look at the attempt at international legal problem-solving through individual national action, including unilateral government action within the framework of bilateral accords governing air travel, landing rights and related matters; national penal laws; administrative and police control measures; private pressure group action by airport trade unions and similar organizations. This enables some sort of quantification of the social costs and gains of these particular, alternative methods of international legal problem-solving.

For the fourth main subject, we are concerned with the question of remedies—the establishment of preferred community solutions for the aerial piracy problem, looking both to the policy choices and also to the machinery-instrumental options. This means trying to establish the main policy alternatives in this general problem area, involving necessarily the creation of some sort of general hierarchy of values, with the relative weight of the "freedom of the air" principle determined in relation, for example, to the principle of "national self-determination". This particular style of approach requires making the link between ends and means in the aerial hijacking problem-area; for policies that are acceptable in community terms when pursued by certain means may be completely unacceptable when pursued by other, quite different means. Our inquiry here takes us necessarily into questions of ultimate legal philosophy—of absolute and relative values. But the problem-solving dilemma can be demonstrated empirically by looking at some of the solutions attempted,—often on a purely *ad hoc* or trial-and-error basis,—in concrete problem-situations involving aerial hijacking, in the international public and international private arenas, and also within individual nation-states by national governments and national courts and private associations and individuals.

The final discussions attempt some sort of a balance-sheet of the various international legal problem-solving ventures in regard to aerial hijacking, particularly over the period since 1960 when the wave of "Cuban" hijackings began and when other, more novel recourses to the diversion of aircraft also arose. The relative merits of holistic or global solutions on the one hand, and a more pragmatic and empirical and particularistic approach on the other are examined, with comparisons made of the concrete record of earlier international attempts, between the two World Wars, at universal solutions in the cognate area of international terrorism. We may be enabled, in this way, to decide operationally whether the international lawyer's prime obligation is to solve a particular problem even if on a limited basis; or whether (and under what circumstances) he is entitled to jeopardize or even abandon solutions of the particular problem in the interests of vindicating some more general and necessarily more high level and abstract, general principles of international law.

Burnaby Mountain, Vancouver — Edward McWhinney
August, 1974

CHAPTER 1

THE NATURE OF THE PROBLEM AND ITS DEFINITION

1. Aerial Piracy or Hijacking of Aircraft: Herein of Special Legal Nomenclature

Aerial piracy—the term popularly, if somewhat inaccurately,[1] ap-

---

1. For the definition of *Piracy* under classical international law, see the well-known *dictum* of Story J. of the US Supreme Court, in *U.S.* v. *Smith,* 5 Wheat. 153, 160-161 (1820):

> "...Whatever may be the diversity of definitions, in other respects, all writers concur in holding that robbery, or forcible depredations upon the sea, *animo furandi,* is piracy. ... The common law, too, recognises and punishes piracy as an offence, not against its own municipal code, but as an offence against the law of nations (which is part of the common law), as an offence against the universal law of society, a pirate being deemed an enemy of the human race."

And see also *In re Piracy Jure Gentium,* (1934) A.C. 586; *Harvard Research in International Law,* "Piracy", 26 *Am.J. Int.L. Supp.* 739 (1932); W. Abendroth, "Piraterie", in Strupp-Schlochauer, *Wörterbuch des Völkerrechts,* Vol. 2 (1962), p. 768.

The United Nations Conference on the Law of the Sea, in its Geneva Convention on the High Seas, 1958, contained certain provisions as to—"piracy on the high seas or in any other place outside the jurisdiction of any State", imposing on all States a duty to—"co-operate to the fullest possible extent in the repression of piracy" (Article 14). The Convention goes on to essay a definition of "piracy" and specifically extends it to cover aircraft as well as ships:

> "Article 15. Piracy consists of any of the following acts:
>
> "(1) Any illegal acts of violence, detention or any act of depredation, committed for private ends by the crew or the passengers of a private ship or a private aircraft, and directed:
>
> "*(a)* On the high seas, against another ship or aircraft, or against persons or property on board such ship or aircraft;
>
> *(b)* Against a ship, aircraft, persons or property, in a place outside the jurisdiction of any State."

Article 19 of the Geneva Convention on the High Seas gives to every State the right, on the high seas, or in any other place outside the jurisdiction of any State, to—

> "Seize a private ship or aircraft, or a ship taken by piracy and under the control of pirates, and arrest the persons and seize the property on board."

The difficulty with the possible application of the Geneva Convention on the High Seas to the illegal diversion of aircraft lies in the quite specific elements

plied to the illegal diversion by force or other means, of an aircraft to a destination other than that envisaged in its original flight plan—is a peculiarly contemporary legal problem. We do not mean this only in the more immediately obvious, or trite, sense that it is, by definition, a delict or crime arising in the air age; but in the more comprehensive sense that it is rendered possible or at least enormously facilitated by the extraordinary complexity of the technological revolution that prepared the way for the post-industrial society, and by the consequent increasing interdependence of all elements of that post-industrial society itself. In the general movement from what the great French so-

---

of the definition of "piracy" contained in Article 15,—in particular, the specification that the acts concerned are to be committed "for private ends", which would seem effectively to exclude any contemporary examples where there is a dominant political motive; and the specification that the acts are to be committed "against another ship or aircraft ...". None of the Cold War, or "Cuban", or Middle East and Mediterranean, cases of illegal diversion of aircraft, cited below, would appear to fall within the definition under Article 15. *Annuaire de l'Institut de droit international,* Vol. 54, I ("Hijacking of Aircraft") (1971), pp. 520 *et seq.*

The difficulties inherent in any attempt at analogical extension of the classical international law as to piracy (whether customary or conventional) to cover the new problem of illegal diversion of aircraft are very well indicated in H. Valladão, "Piraterie aérienne: nouveau délit international", in McWhinney and Bradley (Editors), *The Freedom of the Air* (1968), p. 226; P. de La Pradelle, "Les détournements d'aéronefs et le droit international", *Revue générale de l'air et de l'espace,* Vol. 32 (1969), p. 249; H. van Panhuys, "Aircraft Hijacking and International Law", *Columbia Journal of Transnational Law,* Vol. 9 (1970), pp. 1, 4. And see also S. Shubber, "Is Hijacking of Aircraft Piracy in International Law?", *British Year Book of International Law,* Vol. 43 (1970), p. 193; S. Malik, "Legal Aspects of the Problem of Unlawful Seizure of Aircraft", *Indian Journal of International Law,* Vol. 9 (1969), p. 61; Sir R. Wilberforce, "Crime in Aircraft", *Journal of the Royal Aeronautical Society,* Vol. 67 (1963), p. 175; J. C. Sampaio de Lacerda, "La piraterie aérienne, ses aspects actuels et futurs", *Revue française de droit aérien,* Vol. 24 (1970), p. 281; G. R. Baccelli, "Pirateria Aerea: Realtá effectiva e disciplina giuridica", *Il Diritto Aereo,* Vol. 9 (1970), p. 150; Sergio M. Carbone, "Repressione della c.d. pirateria aerea nei rapporti internazionali", *Rivista di diritto internazionale privato e processuale* (1971), p. 534; A. Crivellaro, "Ancora sulla cosiddetta pirateria aerea: il testo definitivo della Convenzione dell'Aga", *Giurisprudenza italiana* (1972), p. 3; E. Mapelli y Lopez, "Consideraciones sobre la extorsion de aeronaves", *Il Diritto Aereo,* Vol. 8 (1969), p. 261; G. N. Barrie, "Crimes Committed Aboard Aircraft", *South African Law Journal,* Vol. 85 (1968), p. 203; M. de Juglart, "Infractions commises a bord aéronefs dans la doctrine internationale", *Revue française de droit aérien,* Vol. 14 (1960), p. 123; G. Kaminski, " 'Luftpiraterie': die rechtliche beurteilung der an Bord von Luftfahrzeugen begangenen Straftaten unter besonderer der 'Luftpiraterie' ", *Österreichische Zeitschrift für Aussenpolitik,* Vol. 10 (1970), p. 78; S. K. Agrawala, *Aircraft Hijacking and International Law* (1973).

ciologist, Durkheim, identified as the simple, *mechanical* solidarity of early years to an *organic* solidarity based on specialisation of function with resultant interdependence of social or industrial operations,[2] a break at any point in the chain or sequence of events can cause sudden and far-reaching community paralysis. A strike of elevator operators or telephone switchboard operators in Wall Street, for example, would wreak havoc in New York City's financial district.[3] The modern jet aircraft, in its own special way too, is peculiarly vulnerable to attack by wilful or misguided men, because of its engineering refinements and its general technological sophistication,—to an extent and degree that the earlier, less complicated propeller-driven aircraft never were.

All acts of hijacking of aircraft [4] have one element in common, that they involve, as we have said, the forcible diversion of an aircraft

---

2. E. Durkheim, *De la division du travail social* (1893).

3. The increase of complexity and interdependence decreases the amount of spontaneous understanding and agreement among ordinary men of the measures taken, for each sees less and less of the total process to which it is directed: in the movement from social control traceable, as von Savigny had thought, to a people's inner consciousness, *organic solidarity* becomes a socially disruptive rather than a stabilising force.

Julius Stone, *The Province and Function of Law* (1946), pp. 482 *et seq.*; K. Mannheim, *Man and Society in an Age of Reconstruction. Studies in Modern Social Structure* (1940); and see also Jean-François Revel, "Des sociétés fragiles", *L'Express* (Paris), 11-17 September 1972.

4. *Hijacking* is a term with an originally precise connotation deriving from the "Prohibition" era in modern American history when, by virtue of the Eighteenth Amendment to the US Constitution (proclaimed in 1920 and repealed in 1933), the manufacture, sale, or transportation of intoxicating liquors within the United States, and also the importation of such liquors into the United States, was constitutionally prohibited. Hijacking developed as a refinement to the extra-legal activities of criminal elements in the United States seeking to evade the ban, specifically referring to the holding up or robbery, on the part of one gang of criminals, of illicit alcohol being transported in quantity by another, rival gang of criminals, the term "hijack" being popularly accepted as deriving from the colloquial command usually given by the one gang of criminals to the other group, in the act of hold-up: "Hi, Jack, raise your hands!" *Annuaire de l'Institut de droit international,* Vol. 54, I ("Hijacking of Aircraft") (1971), pp. 520 *et seq.* Another explanation, attributed to H. L. Mencken, makes the command more specific: "Raise your hands high, Jack"; while still another explanation is linked, even further back historically, to the romantic 18th-century brigand or *high*wayman operating on the roads at night with his *jack*-light. Andreas Lowenfeld, *Air Law* (1972), ch. 7, s. 1. 2.

The rich historical associations of the term "hijacking", as applied now to aircraft, are only partially conveyed by the more prosaic French-language phrasing,—"le détournement des aéronefs".

in flight, against the will of its air crew.[5] Yet, on examination, it soon becomes apparent that hijacking of aircraft is not one single problem that is uniform in its main constituent elements, but really a series of different and sometimes not always related problems. The approach to the definition of the problem-area indicates its basic polycentricity, for the various examples, over the years, of hijackings of aircraft, lend themselves readily to classification not merely in space-time terms, but also having regard to the special psychological make-up of the main actors involved and their particular ideological associations or political motivations.

2. *The Polycentricity of the Problem-Situation. The Different Species of Aerial Hijackings* [6]

The first main wave of aerial hijackings commenced after World War II with the inauguration of the Cold War Era, when various people, sometimes military personnel and sometimes civilians—seized military or civilian aircraft to flee from the Communist countries of Eastern Europe so as to claim political asylum in the West. Such "East-West" political escapes have become much more intermittent or isolated as the Cold War has progressively given way to the East-

5. The Convention for the Suppression of Unlawful Seizure of Aircraft (The Hague Convention), signed at The Hague on 16 December 1970, essays a definition in the following terms:

> "Article 1. Any person who on board an aircraft in flight:
>
> *(a)* unlawfully, by force or threat thereof, or by any other form of intimidation, seizes, or exercises control of, that aircraft, or attempts to perform any such act, or
>
> *(b)* is an accomplice of a person who performs or attempts to perform any such act
>
> commits an offence (hereinafter referred to as 'the offence')."

The various national attempts at definition are examined in detail in Chapter 3, *5, (b)* (National penal laws), *infra*.

6. The historical development of aerial hijacking, with particular attention to the different time periods and also to the different categories of acts, is presented in some detail in *Annuaire de l'Institut de droit international,* Vol. 54, I (1971), pp. 520 *et seq.*

The Federal Aviation Administration in Washington, DC, maintains a chronological table of all hijackings, the list indicating, among other things, that there had been more than 30 recorded cases of hijackings before the first "Cuban" hijacking in early 1961; the table is reproduced in A. Lowenfeld, *Air Law* (1972).

West, Big Power *détente*. However, we have seen some examples, in recent years, of persons claiming to be subjected to religious persecution in the Soviet Union and to be barred, in consequence, from obtaining normal exit visas except under arduous financial conditions or penalties,[7] who have tried unsuccessfully or who have actually managed to seize aircraft as a sort of desperate "last resort" means of leaving the Soviet Union.[8] This category of hijackings we may call the "political escape" hijackings, corresponding to the political claims, *bona fide* or otherwise, put forward by those attempting them.

A second category of hijackings we may, without too much hesitation, label as the "lunatic fringe" hijackings. They begin with Fidel Castro's accession to power in Cuba, and the termination of direct diplomatic relations between the United States and Cuba that followed shortly thereafter. Beginning in early 1961, when the first United States civil passenger aircraft was hijacked to Havana, a wave of similar hijackings followed over the decade of the 1960s and, indeed, up to the end of 1972. While some of the early hijackings from the United States to Cuba may have had a *bona fide* political motive, it soon became apparent—as extended psychological studies, in depth, of the perpetrators of abortive hijacking attempts after their apprehension, and of actual hijackers since returned from Cuba and taken into custo-

---

7. See, in this regard, Union of Soviet Socialist Republics: Emigration Decree (Adopted by the Council of Ministers of the USSR, 3 August 1972) (Sobranie postanovlenii Pravitel'stva SSSR (1973), No. 1, item 4). Reproduced in *International Legal Materials,* Vol. 12, No. 2 (March 1973), p. 428. The Soviet restrictions on emigration are effectuated, in the case of persons having high technical or professional training in Soviet institutions and wishing to emigrate abroad, through the mechanism of a graduated emigration tax which seems reminiscent in kind (though not, certainly, in degree of severity) of the special *Auswanderung* "tax" applied by the Nazi *régime* to Jews seeking to leave Germany in the middle and late 1930s, or of the financially confiscatory measures applied by the Castro Government to political opponents permitted to leave Cuba in the 1960s.

8. The Soviet emigration restrictions have produced pressures, in the United States Congress, against any relaxation of tariffs on Soviet imports into the United States and against granting Eximbank credits for US exports to the Soviet Union. See the discussion *against* any such US counter-measures by Harold Berman, "Letters to the Editor", *New York Times,* 2 April 1973; and *for* such US counter-measures, E. Bergman, "Letters to the Editor", *New York Times,* 8 April 1973. The then US representative to the UN Commission on Human Rights, Rita E. Hauser, had seemed to argue for an individual or group right, in such cases, to vindicate that "freedom of movement", supposedly guaranteed under general international law: Hauser, "Letter to the Editor", *New York Times,* 7 January 1971; discussed in McWhinney (editor), *Aerial Piracy and International Law* (1971), pp. 18-19.

dy in the United States, have shown—that for the most part these were emotionally disturbed or mentally unbalanced people with very little political or social awareness, and drawn mainly by the contagion of past example, and the lure of the massive publicity given by the communication media (newspapers, television and radio) to past successful hijacking attempts.[9] It is on the basis of this scientific analysis of the "Cuban" hijackers, as a particular class of social delinquents, that the law enforcement officials of the United States have been able to elaborate the so-called hijacker "personality profile", now so widely used in on-the-ground detection procedures.[10] There is no reason, incidentally, to assume that the "lunatic fringe" personalities do not occur from time to time also among the other categories of hijackers, in which the element of motivation—political-ideological or economic—is normally accepted as the main criterion for purposes of identification and classification.

A third group of hijackings—and the most recent in point of time—may be identified as the "hijacking for profit" or "sky bandit" ("skyjacking") category of delinquency: for the dominant motive, here, has clearly been the expectation or hope of instant, large-scale financial gain for the criminal perpetrator. The sky bandit who proceeds to hold the air crew and passengers to ransom for large sums of money, must, undoubtedly, possess considerable qualities of *sang froid* and also actual physical daring, since successful execution of the hijacking plan will normally require escape by parachute from the

---

9. See, for example D. G. Hubbard, *The Skyjacker: His Flights of Fantasy* (1971). Dr. Hubbard's extended psychiatric interviews with arrested hijackers —some 20 in all—reveal startlingly similar characteristics among all of them: a troubled childhood involving withdrawal, fantasy, and absence of contact with playmates and friends; difficult relations with parents, the father usually being violent and alcoholic and the mother fanatically religious; a deeply felt sense of sexual inadequacy, characterised by inability to relate properly to a sexual partner—fantasies of rape and murder at the moment of holding a gun to a stewardess being extremely common. The resemblances to the emotionally and sexually under-developed political assassins, of recent years, in the United States—Oswald, Sirhan, Bremer, for example—are clear.

One of the more bizarre recent cases of an abortive hijacking attempt concerned a bank hold-up in Brooklyn, New York, designed to secure money for a sex-change operation for the homosexual "wife" (then being held in a psychiatric institution) of the leader of the attempt: the venture was foiled when the FBI arrested the leader and killed an accomplice at the John F. Kennedy International Airport in New York. *New York Times,* 23-27 August 1972.

10. Discussed in detail in Chapter 3, *5, (c),* (i) (National Administrative and Police Control Measures: On-the-ground, pre-flight screening and searches of passengers and luggage), *infra.*

hijacked passenger aircraft, together with the ransom money. As a professional skill group, it has been reasoned, this category of hijackers will normally be composed of ex-army paratroopers or civilian sports parachutists (sky-divers). It is perhaps not surprising that this category of hijacker has acquired a certain degree of perverse public respect, even to the point, in one of the more celebrated cases, of developing into something of a popular folk-hero.[11]

A final group of hijackings, confined in geographical terms essentially to the Middle-Eastern countries or at least to nationals or former nationals of those countries,[12] has clearly, as its prime motive among

---

11. See, for example, the case of the hijacker identified only as "D. B. Cooper", who parachuted from a Northwest Orient Airlines Boeing 727 jet passenger aircraft, on 24 November 1971, somewhere between Seattle, Washington, and Reno, Nevada, with $ 200,000 in ransom money, after holding the air crew and stewardesses as hostage: "Cooper", still unapprehended, has been made the subject of popular song ballads and has given interviews to "underground" newspapers in the United States, indicating that he would "be back in five years, thanks to the Statute of Limitations". *The Berkeley Barb,* San Francisco, 12-18 May 1972.

Earlier romantic projections involving the young Italian-American deserter from the US Marine Corps, Raffaele Minichiello, who hijacked a Trans-World Airlines Boeing 707 between Los Angeles and San Francisco and forced the aircrew to fly him on a 17-hour, five-stop, trip to Rome, allegedly to see his girlfriend, included plans by the Italian film producer, Carlo Ponti, to make a movie about Minichiello, on the score that—"The guilt is not just his (Minichiello's). It is also that of society". The *New York Times* reported that Mr. Ponti's verdict had been widely echoed in other comments in Italy as Italians—"increasingly depicted Minichiello more as a folk hero than as an unbalanced juvenile delinquent". (Reported in *Annuaire de l'Institut de droit international,* Vol. 54, I ("Hijacking of Aircraft") (1971), pp. 520 *et seq*). Minichiello, perhaps benefiting by this popular sympathy wave, was sentenced by an Italian court to 7½ years' imprisonment, but released in May 1971, after serving only 18 months: his record, since his release, reveals chronic instability of temperament and inability to hold steady employment, for after earning his living, successively, as a waiter, day labourer, bartender and nude male photographic model, he made the newspaper headlines again in August 1972, when he brought a law suit against his most recent employer, the Grand Hotel in Rome, which had dismissed him from his job in the hotel's sauna baths after only 10 days' employment. The *International Herald Tribune* (Paris), 11 August 1972; *La Sicilia* (Catania), 10 August 1972.

12. Although this category of "political" hijackings is usually associated, in the public mind, with the spectacular, well-organised and co-ordinated, multiple or group hijackings to the Jordanian desert in September 1970, by Palestine Arab nationalist groups—see, in this regard, C. Rousseau, "Détournement et destruction par des commandos palestiniens de quatre avions commerciaux—deux américains, un suisse et un britannique (6 et 9 septembre 1970)", *Revue générale de droit international public* (1970, No. 4), p. 1018; Aircraft Hijacking, Hearings before the Committee on Foreign Affairs, House of Representatives,

Ninety-first Congress 17, 22, 23 and 30 September 1970) (Washington, DC, 1970)—its progenitors or models can be found much earlier, and also in other regions. On 22 October 1956, five Algerian independence leaders, including M. Ben Bella, were involved in an aerial kidnapping on a flight from Rabat, Morocco, to Tunis: they had been invited by the Sultan of Morocco to a conference at Tunis, and their aircraft, a DC-3 operated by the Chérif Company of Morocco, was intercepted over the High Seas by the French authorities and ordered to land at Algiers, then, of course, still French territory. The Moroccan Government contended that the aircraft was Moroccan and that its diversion, under French orders, to French-held Algiers, constituted an act of piracy and violated the international law as to the freedom of the air: the French Government's international law position, apparently, was that the aircraft, even though operated by a Moroccan company, still retained its French nationality and carried the marks of nationality and registration corresponding to its inscription on the French registry, and could therefore legally be submitted to French police controls over the High Seas. P. de La Pradelle, "L'enlèvement aérien des chefs fellagah", *Revue générale de l'air* (1956) (Vol. 19, No. 1), p. 235; and see also M.-E. Valay, "Le déroutement des aéronefs", *Revue générale de l'air et de l'espace* (1969) (Vol. 32, No. 3), p. 340 at pp. 343-344.

Again, on 30 June 1967, a French ex-convict, Bohdenan, hijacked, in Spanish air space, a small private commercial, British-owned aircraft flown by a British crew, and forcibly diverted the aircraft, with its air crew and passengers who included Congolese ex-Premier Moïse Tschombé, to Algiers, where the Algerian Government proceeded to hold the aircrew and passengers, and the hijacker, in close custody, subjecting them, according to some reports, to ill-treatment (*Le Monde,* Paris, 9 July 1967), and denying them access to their respective national consular authorities in Algiers.

The aircrew and non-political passengers were finally released after three months' detention: M. Tschombé was never released, and died two years later, on 29 June 1969, while still in Algerian custody—of a heart attack, according to the Algerian Government's official announcement. C. Rousseau, "Algérie et Congo-Kinshasa: enlèvement en avion de M. Moïse Tschombé au-dessus des Baléares et détention de l'ancien chef du gouvernement congolais par les autorités algériennes, 30 juin 1967", *Revue générale de droit international public* (1968, No. 1), p. 145; E. du Pontavice, "La piraterie aérienne: notion et effets", *Revue générale de l'air et de l'espace* (1969) (Vol. 32, No. 3), p. 276 at pp. 278-279.

A more recent example of a "political" hijacking—this time on the direct command and initiative of a government having absolutely no legal point of contact with the aircraft, its air crew, or its passengers, involved the order given by the Libyan Government to a BOAC commercial passenger aircraft *en route* from London to Khartoum, to land at Benghazi, Libya, the Libyan Government apparently arranging with the Maltese Government to ensure that the Maltese air control authorities would refuse the aircraft access to the air corridor which would have permitted it to land safely in Rome. Aboard the aircraft were two leaders of the short-lived Socialist *putsch régime* in the Sudan: they were arrested by the Libyan Government immediately on landing in Benghazi, and immediately handed over to the old Sudanese Government (which had succeeded in re-establishing itself), and promptly executed. *Le Devoir* (Montreal), 29 July 1971; The *New York Times* (Sunday), 1 August 1971; *Le Monde* (Paris), 20 August 1971.

a plethora of different motives, the solution or at least continuance of hitherto unresolved international conflicts, by novel or unconventional means.[13] This proceeds on the argument, apparently, that the stalemating or clogging of the normal processes of international legal change through peaceful means, thereby operates to render licit or justifiable what otherwise would clearly be impermissible in conventional or classical international law terms.[14]

These so-called "international terrorist" (or "irregular", "privileged combatancy") hijackings, the incidence or at least the threat of which has been mounting in recent years in view of the apparent spectacular political success of several early attempts, are perhaps the most difficult of all to control. For an effective control would seem to require, in the end, some sort of generally acceptable, or at least generally imposed, final solution to the key political conflicts from which they ultimately stem. Foiling of ransom demands, effectuating the release of the air crew and passengers of the hijacked aircraft, and even physical apprehension of the delinquent hijackers and their punishment by due legal process, may not be enough in themselves to nullify or outweigh the effects of an original hijacking, for which the large-scale international publicity attending the disruption and dislocation of international air transportation and the consequent massive publicity for the political cause in whose name those acts were performed, constituted, no doubt, the prime objective.

---

13. Professor Rousseau identifies as a key event in the progression from simple cases of unlawful diversion of aircraft to which the lot of the passengers and crew was secondary, to straight-out exercises in international blackmail, the decision of the Greek Government, several weeks only before the Middle Eastern hijackings of September 1970, to cede to the pressure of Palestinian terrorists and to release the authors of three attacks perpetrated on Greek territory since December 1968, against Israeli aircraft or installations, this notwithstanding that the perpetrators had already been arrested or condemned under Greek Law. C. Rousseau, *Revue générale de droit international public* (1970, No. 4), p. 1018 at p. 1026.

14. See generally T. Meron, "Some Legal Aspects of Arab Terrorists' Claims to Privileged Combatancy", in S. Shoham (Editor), *Of Law and Man* (1971). And see generally, *The Law of Armed Conflicts* (Carnegie Endowment for International Peace) (1971), pp. 78 *et seq.*; also M. Cherif Bassiouni, "Ideologically Motivated Offences and the Political Offences Exception in Extradition", *De Paul Law Review* (1969, Vol. 19), p. 217; J. W. F. Sundberg, " 'Abu Thalaat'. La guerre contre l'aviation civile internationale", *Revue de droit pénal et de criminologie* (October 1971); *Revue française de droit aérien* (1972, No. 2), p. 1.

3. A Plural Problem-Situation as Demanding Plural Solutions

Our conclusion must be that so far from being one simple, comprehensive problem, aerial hijacking reduces, on examination, to a series of different problems, involving widely different personality profiles or professional backgrounds on the part of the main actors; widely different personal or political motivations on the part of those actors; and, finally, widely different choices of means and techniques for effectuating their intention on the part of the actors, depending in part upon their relative intelligence and technological sophistication and in part upon the immediate results desired to be achieved. By way of example, a "sky bandit" presumably would try to minimise publicity aspects since seeking to escape into anonymity and thus to be able to spend at leisure his ill-gotten ransom monies; where an "international terrorist", by contrast, has absolutely no reason to shun publicity after the event and would normally consider ransom money and similar tangible and concrete "blackmail" satisfactions as secondary to the more intangible and symbolic aspects and the impact on the world publicity media.

It is impossible to avoid the conclusion, in any case, that a complex, polycentric problem-situation, has been treated monolithically for purposes of conventional legal analysis and classification, simply because the often quite distinct and different problems or sub-problems involved within it have found their physical expression and outlet in the one particular, somewhat casual and fortuitous fact—namely the act of hijacking, which is sometimes purely symbolic in character, sometimes quite functional and sometimes a mixture of both; and that the same complex, polycentric problem-situation has also tended to be treated monolithically for purposes of application of international legal problem-solving techniques. The consequence has been to produce an essentially uniform approach to all aspects of the problem-situation that may have both unnecessarily delayed the solution of individual aspects of the problem, for which, from time to time, more immediately viable, particularised and short-range remedies have seemed available and at hand, and also at the same time (and paradoxically), frustrated the achievement of any over-all or comprehensive solution for aerial hijackings. The thesis suggested here is in fact that an all too exclusive preoccupation with the search for one universal, holistic remedy has in fact really militated against the possibility of a general solution, to be achieved by using the same essentially low-level, pragmatic, empirical, problem-oriented, step-by-step methods which yielded such impressive results, in the end, in the area of coexistence and the Soviet-Western *détente*; where, by comparison, in the coexistence dialogue, more absolutistic methods that focussed essentially on establishment of a set of *a priori* postulates in treaty or solemn declaration form, proved to be sterile and unproductive.[15]

15. The issues of basic methodology of international legal problem-solving are discussed more fully in the author's *"Peaceful Coexistence" and Soviet-Western International Law* (1964); and also in *International Law and World Revolution* (1967), and in *Conflit idéologique et ordre public mondial* (1970).

CHAPTER 2

THE "SPECIAL LEGAL COMMUNITY" OF THE AIR. THE MAIN PARTICIPANTS IN THE INTERNATIONAL AIR COMMUNICATIONS PROCESS

International air law is part of general public international law; and the World Community in general has a prime interest in maintaining the freedom and safety of air communications and air transportation, untrammelled by the risks of aerial hijackings, and other crimes of violence, directed against aircraft *en route* to their destination and against those aircraft's passengers and crew. Yet there is also, in the technical, jurisprudential sense used by Stammler,[1] a "special legal community" of the air,—whose membership is determined partly by function, partly by professional expertise, and partly by association or user,—which has tended to assume, by design or by default, and sometimes consciously and willingly and sometimes seemingly most unwillingly, a special responsibility for solution of the problems posed by the proliferation of attempts at illegal diversion of aircraft on the international scene. We can examine the membership in this "special legal community" of the air, and also make some comparative evaluation of their degree of interest in or commitment to solutions in this area, and also of their actual problem-solving capacity or competence, by looking to the principal participants involved in the political-legal follow-up to major cases of aerial hijacking in recent years; and looking also to what those participants actually did or did not do in those actual cases of aerial hijacking.

To be sure, in an increasingly interdependent world, all nation States are concerned today, in some way or other, with aerial transportation; but the degree of national interest in aerial transportation obviously corresponds, in measure, to the degree of direct national economic and political-strategic involvement. Certainly the Big Powers, but also a number of "lesser" powers that happen to be major airline countries too (like the Netherlands, Belgium, the Scandinavian countries, Canada, Australia), clearly have, because of their substantial world-wide investments in aircraft and air routes, a far greater concern

1. See, R. Stammler, *Lehre von dem richtigen Recht* (1902).

than other countries with ensuring the safety and regularity of aerial transportation as a whole. Very many countries, indeed, either have no national airlines engaging in genuinely "international" air transportation, or else lease out the management and operation of their own "national" airline to some other major airline country or else to an airline company based in some other major airline country; and they will normally also hire the aircraft themselves and their aircrew from the same source. This latter group of countries' interest in vindicating the freedom of the air and related principles of international air law will understandably tend to be rather muted or secondary, at least until such time as a concrete incident of aerial hijacking raises other, non-air law clusters of legal principles or legal values—like those having to do with the so-called "irregular" or "privileged combatancy", "national self-determination" and the like,—in which case those particular countries' attitudes, in the resultant conflict of interests, are as likely as not, to be negative or hostile to the major airline countries' general assertion of the supremacy of the air law values. These radically divergent national attitudes, corresponding to the radically different degrees and extent of national investment or involvement in the international air transportation industry, are strikingly reflected in the record of affirmative and negative votes, and also the abstentions, in international intergovernmental arenas that have passed upon the aerial hijacking problem-situation in any one or more of its phases, at particular times; and they are also reflected in the alternative elements of co-operation, or partisan intransigence, or "fence-sitting" disengagement that those individual national votes represent, in practical international problem-solving terms.

1. The United Nations Security Council and General Assembly

The issue of the international legal control of aerial hijacking has been raised in a number of international, inter-governmental arenas, —some of these general, and some specialised in functional terms. The United Nations Security Council and the United Nations General Assembly have both, at various times, passed upon the problem, and they have recorded their opinions in the form of resolutions, which, understandably perhaps because of the political exigencies involved in both arenas in achieving some formula capable of universal, or near universal, adoption, have been formulated only in rather vague and general terms [2]—strong in moral precept, no doubt, but rather weak in terms of operationalism and the offering of any very concrete remedies.[3] Of course it may be argued that, apart from the political sacri-

---

2. Thus the UN General Assembly resolution on Forcible Diversion of Civil Aircraft in Flight (resolution 2551 (XXIV), 12 December 1969), which "*calls upon* States to take every appropriate measure to ensure that their respective national legislations provide an adequate framework for effective legal measures"; and which "*urges* States in particular to ensure that persons on board who perpetrate (hijackings) are prosecuted", and which also "*urges* full support for the efforts of the International Civil Aviation Organization" and "*invites* States to ratify or accede to" the Tokyo Convention of 1963.

Similarly, the UN Security Council resolution on hijacking of aircraft and any other interference in international travel (resolution 286 (1970), 9 September 1970), after expressing "*grave concern*" at the "threat to innocent civilian lives from the hijacking of aircraft", "*appeals*" to all parties concerned for the "immediate release of all passengers and crews (of hijacked aircraft) without exception", and "*calls* on States to take all possible legal steps to prevent further hijackings".

The UN General Assembly resolution on aerial hijacking or interference with civil air travel (resolution 2645 (XXV), 30 November 1970), "*condemns,* without exception whatsoever, all acts of aerial hijacking", and "*calls upon* States to take all appropriate measures to deter, prevent or suppress such acts within their jurisdiction". The resolution also "*declares* that the exploitation of unlawful seizure of aircraft for the purpose of taking hostages is to be condemned", and "*urges* States to provide for the care and safety of (a hijacked aircraft's) passengers and crew and to enable them to continue their journey as soon as practicable and to return the aircraft and its cargo to the persons lawfully entitled to possession"; and ends with an "*invitation*" to States to ratify or accede to the Tokyo Convention of 1963 and to support the efforts of ICAO to counter hijackings.

A further, so-called consensus statement adopted unanimously by the Security Council on 20 June 1972, declared the "*grave concern*" of the Security Council at the threat to the lives of passengers and crews arising from aerial hijackings; "condemn(ed) and consider(ed) it necessary to put an end" to acts of hijacking; and once again "call(ed) upon States to take all appropriate measures within their jurisdiction to deter and prevent" hijackings.

The UN Press release containing the announcement of the Security Council consensus statement included the poignant comment: "Asked by newsmen if members really felt that this would prevent hijacking, the Council President said that preventive measures in this field were not up to the Council, but depended on the political willingness of States to act." (United Nations Press Section, *Weekly News Summary,* Press Release WS/560, 23 June 1972.)

3. By contrast, the Resolutions and Recommendations of international regional organisations such as the Council of Europe are, by reason no doubt of their greater compactness and cohesiveness and also the substantial degree of value homogeneity among their members, very much more precise and concrete and, hence more operational. See, in this regard Council of Europe, Consultative Assembly, Resolution 450 (1970) on air piracy, adopted by the Assembly on 18 September 1970 (10th sitting); and see also Council of Europe Consultative Assembly, Recommendation 613 (1970) on air safety and unlawful seizure of aircraft, adopted by the Assembly on 24 September 1970 (18th sitting). The latter

fices required to achieve the apparent prime *desideratum* of voting unanimity, either body—the Security Council or the General Assembly [4]—would be exceeding its own "special competence" if it ventured upon any very technical or detailed recommendations or stipulations in the air transportation field. On the principle of respect for institutional "*rôles and missions*" adumbrated by Mr. Justice Frankfurter of the United States Supreme Court, there being a specialised international inter-governmental agency already long in existence in the air transportation field, with its immense, accumulated technical expertise and its own back-log of administrative precedents, —namely, the International Civil Aviation Organization (ICAO), it would be constitutionally inelegant, to say the least, for the UN Security Council or the UN General Assembly to attempt to pre-empt or occupy a field falling within the special competence of that agency—at least until such time as that agency had demonstrated itself as being incapable or unwilling to act in any concrete and meaningful way.

Council of Europe Recommendation in particular, after—"noting that organised air terrorism originates in the territory of a small number of States, and that those who are responsible for it seem to enjoy moral and financial support, and even arms supplies from the authorities of certain States",—goes on to urge member States to introduce stricter preventive and control measures over air travellers and luggage at airports, and invites member States to reinforce security measures on board aircraft and to consider placing armed guards on board. The Recommendation also asks the member States to establish sanctions, such as boycotting airports or air companies and refusing landing rights to the airlines operated from States on whose territory organised air terrorism is tolerated or which have refused either to extradite or severely punish offenders.

4. We leave to one side, for the moment, the issue of the normative, law-making quality of UN General Assembly and/or Security Council resolutions, on the score that, except where they may be viewed as simply re-stating already existing customary international law principles—such as, for example, the duty of a State, to whose territory an aircraft is hijacked, to release the aircraft and its aircrew, passengers, and cargo, and speed them on their original journey as soon as possible (and see further, *infra*), the UN General Assembly and Security Council resolutions on hijacking cited above are really formulated at such a high level of generality and abstraction as to be incapable of having normative legal force in particular cases. See generally D. H. N. Johnson, "The Effect of Resolutions of the General Assembly of the United Nations", 32 *British Year Book of International Law* 98 (1955-6); R. Higgins, *The Development of International Law through the Political Organs of the United Nations* (1963); C. Parry, *The Sources and Evidences of International Law* (1965); O. Y. Asamoah, *The Legal Significance of the Declarations of the General Assembly of the United Nations* (1966); I. I. Lukashuk, *Istochniki Mezhdunarodnogo Prava* (1966), especially at pp. 81-94; V. Pechota, "Valne Shromazdeni OSN a Projednavani Pravnich zasad Miroveho Souziti", 7 *Casopis pro Mezinarodni Pravo* 97 (1963).

2. *The International Civil Aviation Organization (ICAO)*

Now the International Civil Aviation Organization [5] itself may also tend from time to time to have problems of special competence, arising from the complex, many-faceted, polycentric problem-situations coming before it. For very many of the problems coming before ICAO in recent years have contained high political elements—going to some of the major political tension-issues of the World Community today—that quite transcend the professional qualifications and experience of the essentially air transportation-oriented, national delegations to ICAO and also, at the same time, of the civil service staff and advisors within the ICAO secretariat itself. Though the professional qualifications and experience available within the ICAO family may be of high quality, it is, of necessity, a somewhat narrow, essentially technically based expertise that is shaped and controlled in the end by the somewhat narrow, essentially technically based, air transportation problems with which ICAO has been concerned since its formation in 1947. In the case of ICAO, not less than with other UN specialised agencies—notably, also, the International Telecommunication Union (ITU),[6]—the original function inevitably tends to determine not merely the nature and form of the actual policy-making, but also the basic personality type called upon to make the key decisions involved. Over a period of years, a particular, specialised function-based bureaucratic personality may become ingrained and self-perpetuating within a particular international agency, with results that are no doubt fully beneficial in so far

5. On ICAO generally, Walter Binaghi, "The *rôle* of ICAO", in E. McWhinney and M. A. Bradley (editors), *The Freedom of the Air* (1968), pp. 17-29; R. H. Mankiewicz, "L'Organisation de l'aviation civile internationale", *Annuaire français de droit international,* Vol. 13 (1967), p. 482; J. Erler, *Rechtsfragen der ICAO. Die Internationale Zivilluftfahrtorganisation und ihre Mitgliedstaaten* (1967); T. Buergenthal, *Law-making in the International Civil Aviation Organisation* (1969); *Shawcross and Beaumont on Air Law* (P. B. Keenan, A. Lester, P. Martin (editors) (3rd edition, 1966); N. M. Motte, *Traité de droit aérien-aéronautique* (2nd ed., 1964).

6. See, in this regard, H. K. Jacobson, "International Institutions for Telecommunications. The ITU's *Rôle*", in E. McWhinney (editor), *The International Law of Communications* (1971), p. 51; Gordon L. Weil, *Communicating by Satellite* (20th Century Fund), New York (1969), pp. 4-11; W. R. Hinchman and D. A. Dunn, *The Future of Satellite Communications* (20th Century Fund), New York (1970), pp. 21-27; Simone Courteix, "L'Union internationale des télécommunications (UIT) et son rôle dans le domaine des télécommunications spatiales", in *Les télécommunications par satellites, aspects juridiques* (C.-A. Colliard and A.-Ch. Kiss (editors) (1970)), p. 245.

as the continuance and development of existing lines of decision within that agency's area of special competence may be concerned; but with somewhat more questionable consequences when revolutionary new problems arise that may challenge the very premises upon which the agency itself was originally founded. The hiatus—really a time-lag—between the settled expectations of an agency's political and administrative "establishments", based on their own precedents developed over the years—and the revolutionary new problems, is perhaps to be seen in the case of the ITU in that agency's difficulties in adjusting from an original, "posts and telegraphs" historical identity and personality, to the dramatic problems posed today by the unprecedented transformation of international telecommunications with the development of satellite television broadcasting,—these new problems calling for a new range of policy decisions, covering all the technical exigencies imposed by advanced communications science and technolgy, and balanced by the free speech *versus* thought control considerations thought to be inherent in a situation where control of the communication media is in the hands of one or two large and only imperfectly competing corporations or else of the government alone.

There is, as Dewey noted, a terminal value inherent in old ideas; in the political-administrative area, a bureaucratic momentum can carry along old policy constructs and thought-ways long after the original societal conditions that gave birth to and justified them have disappeared. In the case of ICAO, an adjustment has sometimes been attempted to be made *ad hoc* and on a crash basis, to radically new problems, by blending the ideologues or "political generalists" into the normal national delegations to ICAO, for the specific purpose of debate on a particular political tension-issue that has suddenly come up, in the interstices of the normal ICAO "air-transportation" agenda. But it may be argued that such emergency, *ad hoc* remedies have actually increased ICAO's difficulties in arriving at rational problem-solving by "politicising" the process of decision itself, and thereby producing an undue emphasis upon polemics and the taking of debating points and cheap personalities that have hitherto been lacking in the ICAO debates as a whole. Episodes like the angry, vituperative debates over the Israeli "reprisal" commando bombing of the Beirut International Airport in 1968, or over the more recent shooting-down of the Libyan civil aircraft that had transgressed the airspace over the Israeli-occupied Sinai Peninsula, are unhappy examples of the practical consequences of trying to mix together "functional" expertise and "ideological" expertise (and, of course to mix together also the particular national experts specialised in their respective practice), in the one international problem-solving venture. So far as these "new" international law problems tend to exceed the traditional special competence of a specialised international inter-governmental agency like ICAO, it may be contended that, rather than trying to solve those problems within the confines of that specialised agency and so running the risk of perverting the specialised agency from its original historical purpose, it would be better to refer them, as high "political" problems, to the United Nations proper, as more appropriate for decision by the World Community as a whole. If the United Nations Security Council and the General Assembly should then themselves either return the compliment by referring those same problems back to ICAO, on the argument of their basic, "air transportation" component, or else attempt to discharge their own burden of public responsibility in the matter by a deliberately vague or woolly resolution that in no way faces up to the real issues in the case, then there may be no solution but for the specialised agency to try radically to adjust its own methods and techniques and personnel to solution of the problem. In effect, then, one must "radicalise" the specialised agency to resolve the radically new problem—something that, so far, no United Nations specialised agency has seemed really able or willing to do for itself. It may, therefore, be unfair to single out ICAO as having a responsibility of reforming itself, by auto-gestion as it were, in order to solve the revolutionary new "political" air law problems of an era of ideological contestation.

3. *The International Air Transport Association (IATA)*

Another main member of the "special legal community" of the air is the International Air Transport Association (IATA), an international private association of the major commercial airline companies of the world, both the privately owned and the wholly State (governmentally owned and operated) airlines.[7] The continuing existence of IATA is another tribute to the complex, polycentric character of the system of world public order as applied to civil aviation. In the absence

7. On IATA generally, see K. Hammarskjöld, "The *Rôle* of IATA", in *The Freedom of the Air* (1968), p. 30; Sir William Hildred, "The Interdependence of ICAO and IATA", in *The Freedom of the Air* (1968), p. 40.

of any widespread international agreement, at the time of the drafting of the Chicago Convention of 1944,[8] on over-arching intergovernmental machinery covering air routes, rates, and traffic rights for international scheduled airlines, these matters had to be omitted altogether from the Chicago Convention and left, in the end, to action on the part of individual governments with each other.

In the result, there developed a multitude of special intergovernmental, bilateral air transport agreements.[9] Yet in the majority of these bilateral agreements reference will be found, directly or indirectly, to IATA as the machinery through which rates, fares and charges are to be negotiated by air carriers. At the beginning of 1967 there were 1,248 bilateral air transport agreements in existence between over 100 nations, and of this number no less than 872 referred to IATA as the machinery for fare and rate negotiation. The prime instrument within IATA for securing such arrangements is IATA's Traffic Conference machinery. The function of the Traffic Conference is to promulgate resolutions, which are themselves subject to approval by participating governments, these resolutions being designed to establish fares, rates, charges and rules and regulations for scheduled international air services. All Traffic Conference agreements must be reached by unanimous vote, which, in effect, gives a veto power to every airline, regardless of size, in the Conference of which it is a member. To the outside observer it may sometimes appear that IATA has operated as a cartel and kept fares on the most profitable air transportation routes well above the levels that pure commercial-costing calculations might warrant.[10] Yet IATA has filled the vacuum as to

8. See the author's "International Law and the Freedom of the Air. The Chicago Convention and the Future", *Rutgers-Camden Law Journal,* Vol. 1 (1969), p. 229; A. A. Berle, "The Air Transportation Crisis and the Future", in *The Freedom of the Air* (1968), p. 13; M. Pourcelet, "The International Element in Air Transport", *Journal of Air Law and Commerce,* Vol. 33 (1967), p. 75; P. H. Sand, "The International Unification of Air Law", *Law and Contemporary Problems* (1965), p. 400.

9. Francis Déak, "The Balance-Sheet of Bilateralism", in *The Freedom of the Air* (1968), p. 159; Whitney Gillilland, "Bilateral Agreements", in *The Freedom of the Air* (1968), p. 140.

10. See the testimony by the then Director-General of IATA, Sir William Hildred, before the Antitrust Subcommittee of House Judiciary Committee, US Congress, in 1956, reproduced in A. Chayes, T. Ehrlich, and A. F. Lowenfeld, *International Legal Process: Materials for an Introductory Course* (1968), pp. 516-522; A. F. Lowenfeld, *Aviation Law. Cases and Materials* (1972), Ch. 3. And see K. G. J. Pillai, *The Air Net. The Case against the World Aviation Cartel* (1969).

direct multilateral governmental control under the Chicago Convention; and IATA's network of bilateral arrangements is, in many respects, a necessary complement to the positive law of the Chicago Convention. IATA and ICAO are, in a practical sense, therefore, interdependent and complementary. In a juristic sense, IATA is, as we have noted, an international private, commercial association that is limited, in terms of sanctions for effectiveness, to any penalties (including expulsion from membership), available within its own internal administrative procedures and also to those private law-based, contractual-type remedies for which recourse may exist on an ordinary Conflicts of Law basis. Nevertheless, the formal link so repeatedly made between the plethora of individual, bilateral air transport agreements between different States and the IATA fare and rate-fixing machinery, does seem, in the United States Supreme Court's phrase, to "affect with the public interest" IATA and its various operations and so give a sort of public international law infra-structure to them,—thus rendering public what would otherwise of course be strictly private.

As a member of the "special legal community" of the air and so a potentially important participant in the international law-making process as to control of aerial hijacking, IATA has largely limited itself to the passing of essentially hortatory resolutions calling upon people other than itself—for example, the United Nations and its agencies, governments—to take criminal and other action against hijackers; and to some measures for co-ordination of research and exchange of information between airlines as to preventive, on-the-ground security measures.[11] IATA has signally eschewed all the opportunities seemingly presented by its own "airline club" character, of mounting psychological and also, and more importantly, economic pressures against

11. The Director-General of IATA, on 23 February 1970, following on the fatal bomb explosion which destroyed a Swissair aircraft in flight and a similar bomb explosion on board an Austrian Airlines aircraft, called for increased protection at airports, particularly at transit airports which he described as the "weak links in the chain of counter actions". On 9 March 1970, the Executive Committee of IATA called for reinforced measures directed against the "proliferation of aggression against civil aircraft"—in particular, for co-ordination of airport security amongst all interested agencies (postal authorities, customs, immigration, local police); for scientific screening measures to be applied to all passengers, baggage, cargo, and airmail; and for maximum exchange of information on security. Cited in *Annuaire de l'Institut de droit international*, Vol. 54, I ("Hijacking of Aircraft") (1971), pp. 520 *et seq*.

the airlines of "delinquent" States that welcome or otherwise harbour and encourage aerial hijackers, through the threat of expulsion from IATA, or through other forms of internal "club" penalties operating through the complicated fare and rate structures established under IATA's special Traffic Conference machinery. Since the overwhelming intellectual commitment of IATA's members and its key officers to the principle of control of aerial hijacking is clear, one is left with two main alternative conclusions from the IATA record of substantial inactivity of a concrete, operational character in regard to control of hijacking: either that, when the crunch came, IATA's members preferred, for purely selfish economic reasons not to jeopardise continuance of profitable airline route privileges by the application of politically divisive sanctions actions against a few, largely government-owned airlines whose home governments were "soft" on hijacking; or else that, on the example of ICAO before it, IATA and its members preferred, somewhat uncourageously perhaps, to restrict themselves to the narrow area of their own special competence—fare and rate-fixing—leave the difficult, politically and ideologically based problems for solution by the main political organs of the World Community—the UN Security Council and General Assembly—or not at all.

4. The International Federation of Airline Pilots Associations (IFALPA)

The airline pilots, as represented institutionally by the International Federation of Airline Pilots Associations [12] and by the various constituent national Airline Pilots Associations, has been perhaps the most continuingly vocal member of the "special legal community" of the air on the issue of the need to control aerial hijacking; and it has certainly been the one most inclined towards the taking of direct action—concrete measures that really do have some teeth in them, to be applied to "delinquent" States that render aid or comfort to hijackers, either before or after the act of hijacking. But then the airline pilots do have a direct and immediate, and personal interest in control of aerial hijacking. The pilots fly their planes almost every day and the mathematical chances, therefore, of the aircraft under

12. On IFALPA, see I. M. Shepard, "Air Piracy: the *Rôle* of the International Federation of Airline Pilots Associations", *Cornell International Law Journal,* Vol. 3 (1970), p. 79; G. Horlick, 12 *Harvard International Law Journal* 33.

their control being illegally diverted during flight; or of the pilots themselves being assaulted and injured or killed on the ground or in flight or being held hostage or otherwise physically maltreated by some foreign government after the hijacked aircraft has been diverted there and the hijackers themselves given political haven, are very much greater and certainly more immediate than the chances of a similar evil fate befalling the diplomats who go as delegates to UN General Assembly or ICAO Council meetings or the private airline company executives (or high bureaucrats, in the case of government-owned commercial airlines) who take part in the IATA reunions. These latter categories of persons, after all, may need to use an airline only once or twice a month on average, and so the risks of their being waylaid *en route* may be reasonably tolerable to the persons concerned. It is perhaps understandable, therefore, that the airline pilots, as a special skill group undergoing constant exposure to the hazards of aerial hijacking, may show little patience with those in other international arenas who seek to balance the need for effective criminal law controls against the traditional, classical international law category of political asylum; or, even more, against claimed civil liberties of the criminal hijacker which are asserted by some liberal constitutional thinkers. In pressing for direct action, the airline pilots seem well warranted, experientially, in concluding that direct action is an effective form of control of the problem of aerial hijacking: in the single case, occurring in 1968, of application of direct action, through threat of boycott, on the part of all members of IFALPA, of flights into and out of a delinquent host country that had first given haven to hijackers and that had then gone on to hold the hijacked aircraft and its air crew and most of its passengers for six weeks after the original hijacking, the host country concerned, Algeria, when threatened with such boycott, immediately gave way and released aircraft, air crew, and passengers.[13]

13. On 23 July 1968, a Boeing 707 jet airliner, owned and operated by El Al Airlines of Israel, on a flight from Rome to Tel Aviv and while still in Italian air space, was hijacked by Palestinian Arab terrorists and forcibly diverted to Algiers. The Algerian authorities almost immediately released the non-Israeli passengers. Then, after some days, the women and children among the Israeli passengers were released. Finally, after 6 weeks, and following IFALPA's public threat to place a boycott on all flights by its members into Algeria, the remaining 5 male Israeli passengers and the 7 Israeli crew members were permitted to return to Rome, their original place of departure, on an Alitalia aircraft. The El Al aircraft was then flown out of Algiers to Rome, by an Air France crew. Cited in *Annuaire de l'Institut de droit international,* Vol. 54, I ("Hijacking of Aircraft") (1971), pp. 520 *et seq.*

IFALPA has, however, never again applied a similar measure,—perhaps because of veiled pressures upon the individual pilots making up the IFALPA membership, exercised by the airline companies employing the pilots; perhaps because of doubts on the part of the individual pilots themselves as to whether they might not be in breach of their personal contracts of service in refusing to fly an aircraft into or out of a particular country designated by their airline companies. Since that time, IFALPA and its constituent national units have limited themselves, like IATA and its constituent commercial airline companies, to essentially hortatory resolutions addressed to persons other than themselves. Measures such as the well-publicised 24-hour, global strike of airline pilots, which are designed, in the words of IFALPA as expressed in its March 1969 special resolution entitled, "Freedom of Transit—Hijacking of Civil Aircraft" [14]—"to focus public attention on this most pressing problem of air safety"—may, because of the resulting measure of inconvenience to the travelling general public, and perhaps also because of the element of direct financial loss to the commercial airlines affected by the strike, yield some greater practical results than the normal mere "solemn resolution", favoured by the International Civil Aviation Organisation (ICAO), in terms of spurring concrete action on the part of international inter-governmental agencies, national governments, and the commercial airline cartels. But these measures do not seem intrinsically different, nevertheless, from the "solemn resolutions" based approach to control of aerial hijacking. For they do not, in themselves, yield practical results; since a further follow-up initiative is needed to translate them into concrete action, and that usually on the part of persons other than the actual sponsors of those "solemn resolutions".

5. The Individual Passenger

A final, and too often overlooked member of the "special legal community" of the air is the individual private passenger. To be sure, UN General Assembly delegates, ICAO Council members, IATA dignitaries, and airline pilots are also individual private passengers from time to time. But the difference is that in their main contact with the aerial hijacking problem these other people can usually bring to bear

14. Cited in *Annuaire de l'Institut de droit international,* Vol. 54, I ("Hijacking of Aircraft") (1971), pp. 520 *et seq.*

all the weight of some well-organised and well-financed political-governmental institution, or pressure group or private association. The individual private passenger, by contrast, is all alone in the matter. On the whole, he has co-operated, with good humour, in the on-the-ground searches of his person and his hand luggage and his aircraft hold baggage; and this usually without any protest as to the constitutional law, "illegal search and seizure" aspects [15] of those control measures. For the individual private passenger will either not know about such esoteric constitutional law questions; or, if he does know, he will tend to conclude that they should sensibly be subordinated to considerations of the safety and security of the aircraft and its air crew and its passengers. If the individual private passenger should end up being physically injured or emotionally shocked as a result of a hijacking action; or if he should end up, against his will, in some distant city or burning desert, where he may remain for some indefinite time as an innocent pawn in some grandiose international blackmail venture or similar power political play, what can he do when he eventually reaches safety again, if he should be so fortunate as to come through the misadventure with his life? Remembering the classical Western constitutional law notion—through Dicey—of legal rights as finding their ultimate foundation and source in free-willing individuals' direct initiatives to vindicate those rights in individual private legal actions, our individual private passenger can always, on his return to safety, bring a personal legal action for damages against the airline company that had originally contracted to carry him to his designated destination, such personal legal actions being based on breach of the original contract for safe carriage, and also on liability in delict (negligence) on the part of the airline company.[16] (The individual private passenger's practical possibility of a private legal action, in delict, against the criminal delinquents who hijacked him in the first place is presumably effectively foreclosed by the fact that those delinquents will have disappeared, by now, into the country that offered them haven in the first place and

15. *US Constitution, Bill of Rights,* Article IV: "The right of the people to be secure in their persons, houses, papers, and effects, against unreasonable searches and seizures, shall not be violated, and no Warrants shall issue, but upon probable cause, supported by Oath or affirmation, and particularly describing the place to be searched, and the persons or things to be seized."

The application of this provision is discussed in detail in Chapter 3, *5, (c),* (i), *infra.*

16. See, for example, *Husserl* v. *Swiss Air Transport Company Ltd.,* 351 F. Supp. 702 (1972); discussed in detail in Chapter 3, *6, infra.*

so be unavailable for service of legal process.) In proceeding against the airline company that had originally contracted to carry him to his designated destination, the individual passenger faces certain hurdles, both practical and also doctrinal-legal. As a practical matter, a private suit in damages against a large commercial corporation is terribly worrying and time-consuming and also terribly expensive. It may have seemed to Dicey, and to other late 19th-century constitutional theorists, as an ideal remedy for the vindicating of constitutional rights on the part of the politically self-reliant and sophisticated intellectual *élite* of the classical liberal democratic society; but it just does not tend to work out that way today. And from the viewpoint of strict legal doctrine, there remain some major and as yet unresolved issues such as the extent to which traditional principles of liability are affected or controlled by the Warsaw Convention and related instruments; and also the applicability or otherwise of traditional legal defences of the nature of Act of God, as incorporated into liability-excluding clauses in contracts of carriage. The path ahead for the individual private passenger who determines to be a good citizen and to seek to vindicate himself, by his own personal legal action, the principle of "the freedom of the air", where international agencies, governments and private pressure groups and associations have, by contrast, signally failed to move effectively in that area, is a difficult one; though the rewards, if the individual private passenger should prove in the end to be successful, are likely—on past experience, with cognate legal problems—to be substantial in financial terms, at least in those jurisdictions that permit jury verdicts on the actions. For the general public, when sitting as members of juries in civil cases, has usually shown a keen regard for the practical possibilities of compelling airline companies to maintain high safety standards by imposing on them stiff financial penalties in case of apparent default in their public responsibilities.

CHAPTER 3

THE TECHNIQUES OF INTERNATIONAL LEGAL PROBLEM-SOLVING AS APPLIED TO AERIAL HIJACKING

The techniques of international legal problem-solving are, of course, many and varied. Some methods, such as the two-nation, bilateral treaty, or else the more limited regional pact, are obviously particularly suited to the solution of problems that tend to be confined to one particular geographical area only, where the parties concerned are likely to have a common interest in solution. And this type of agreement is undoubtedly easiest to achieve and certainly most likely to be operational where the parties concerned have a common ideological base, as for example, with those Western European countries joined by treaty into the European Community. Sometimes where a problem is peculiarly complex and difficult in terms of its technical components, so that the attempt to include large numbers of parties in an agreement would be likely to produce only a long-delayed and unwieldy document, the problem may best be solved by the route of the bilateral treaty, the first such treaty serving as a model for innumerable subsequent treaties, so that, in the end, we have a series of more or less interlocking treaties that, in their sum, may present all the advantages of universality of a multilateral treaty, but perhaps also the additional advantage, secured by the more intensive and concentrated method of negotiation involved in bilateral treaties, of greater relative precision and concreteness as to objectives.

In the post-World War II era, the treaty has certainly, in quantitative terms at least, become the prime source of international law. It has also become the favoured instrument for international lawmaking in the era of the Big Power (bipolar) *détente,* as the Soviet Union and the United States moved to mutal accommodation of interests in a series of concrete problem-situations.[1] In such cases, it has been the bilateral

1. As to the relative primacy of the Treaty as a source of contemporary International Law, and as to its favoured position in Soviet-US bilateral accommodations, leading on to the Soviet-US *détente,* see generally the author's *"Peaceful Coexistence" and Soviet-Western International Law* (1964).

treaty that has been used; with the original accord often (as in the case of the Partial Nuclear Test Ban Treaty of August 1963), worked out jointly by the Soviet Union and the United States at a Summit Meeting and then subsequently opened up to other, secondary powers, for signature, though without any right of amendment or qualification on the part of those other powers.

In the case of the control of aerial hijacking, a joint Soviet-United States impetus to solution of the problem was originally lacking. The Soviet Union only latterly became interested in the international institutional arrangements and formal international organisation as to air law to the point of actually applying for membership in ICAO. [2] For after some early, Cold War era, incidents of hijacking of aircraft from the Soviet Union (possibly sponsored by Western intelligence services), the Soviet Union had not been again seriously troubled by hijackings until several decades later when several *causes célèbres* arose involving Soviet citizens,[3] sometimes claiming to be subject to

---

2. The Soviet Government first gave notice of its adherence to the Chicago Convention of 1944, on 15 October 1970, and thus became an ICAO Contracting State as of 14 November 1970, the Soviet Union being the 120th member of ICAO. *ICAO News Release,* Montreal (November 1970); *Pravda,* Moscow, 28 November 1970.

3. *Pravda* of 16 October 1970, and *Izvestiya* of 17 October 1970, carried reports of the hijacking of a Soviet civil passenger AN-24 aircraft, on 15 October 1970, while on a flight from Batumi to Sukhumi, two armed bandits (father and son), having killed the aircraft's stewardess and wounded the two pilots and forced the aircraft to change course and land in Trabzon, Turkey: the same reports indicated that the Soviet Government had asked the Turkish authorities to extradite the two criminal hijackers so that they could be tried in a Soviet court, and also to return the aircraft and the air crew and passengers. *Pravda* of 20 October 1970, reported that a Turkish court of original jurisdiction in Trabzon had declined the Turkish state prosecutor's request for issuance of a warrant for the arrest of the two hijackers; and spoke of certain groups in Turkey, interested in impeding good-neighbour relations between the Soviet Union and Turkey, who were attempting to persuade Turkish public opinion that the Soviet demand for extradition of the hijackers was a blow to Turkish dignity. *Izvestiya* of 21 October 1970, announced the return of the plane and its passengers to the Soviet Union, and severely criticised the Turkish authorities for postponing the issue of extradition, and for setting up a protective field around the hijackers by representing them as having acted out of political motives and to be seeking political asylum.

Izvestiya of 1 January 1971, reported the arrest and trial of 11 persons for an abortive attempt to hijack a Soviet civil passenger AN-2 aircraft at Smolny airport in Leningrad on 15 June 1970, and to fly it to Boden in Sweden. The 11 persons were given sentences of imprisonment ranging down from 15 years for the three leaders, to 4 years. *Izvestiya,* in publishing the report, was at the same time sharply critical of Zionist activities in the United States; and *Pravda*

persecution within the Soviet Union on account of their religious beliefs, who allegedly became involved in hijacking acts or their preparation.[4] Lacking the catalyst of a joint, Soviet-US sponsored com-

---

of 1 January 1971, in carrying a similar story, reported that Zionist groups in the West were taking advantage of the Jewish nationality of some of the convicted persons to create the impression that the Soviet court had tried them for their nationality and not for the crime of hijacking.

Pravda and *Izvestiya* of 21 September 1972 reported the public trial of two persons accused of seizing an Aeroflot L-200 aircraft in October 1970, on a flight from Kerch to Krasnodar, and forcibly diverting it to Turkey: the reports said that, under an agreement with the Turkish Government, the two hijackers were returned to the Soviet Union, and that, on their conviction, they were severely punished, and that the verdict had been greeted with great approval in the court-room. The *New York Times* of 16 September 1972 had earlier reported the trial and convictions of these two hijackers, claiming that they had been given prison terms of 13 years and 10 years respectively, and that, though they had requested political asylum in Turkey, Turkey had turned them over to the Soviet Union, after a year: the *New York Times* also reported that the two earlier (father and son) hijackers who had forcibly diverted a Soviet aircraft to Turkey on 15 October 1970, were still in Turkey and understood to be facing trial there. The *New York Times* report claimed to have picked up the news of the convictions and sentences in the present hijacking case—prior to its publication in *Pravda* and *Izvestiya*—from a local, Crimean paper; and that the Soviet authorities were unwilling to give wide publicity to hijackings because Soviet citizens can leave the Soviet Union "only with special permission and many people have been frustrated in efforts to emigrate". (*New York Times,* 16 September 1972.)

The *New York Times* of 6 May 1973 reported that Soviet officials had privately confirmed that a Soviet citizen killed himself and a Soviet airline pilot on 24 April 1973 after an unsuccessful attempt to hijack a TU-104 Aeroflot civil aircraft on a flight from Leningrad to Mosow, and to divert it to Stockholm: when the pilot landed, instead, at Leningrad, the hijacker apparently triggered a bomb, killing himself and the pilot.

4. The mounting Soviet official concern with the problem of hijacking is evidenced both in the Soviet scientific legal literature and also in a series of official actions. See, for example, *Pravda,* 4 December 1970, reporting favourably on the ICAO conference at The Hague to draft a new convention concerning prevention of hijackings of aircraft; *Pravda,* 28 November 1970, containing an article by O. Khlestov praising the UN General Assembly resolution 2645 (XXV), 1970; *Izvestiya* of 16 January 1971, containing a further article by O. Khlestov praising the Hague Convention of December 1970.

And see also P. Yevseyev and Yu. Kolosov, "Air Bandits Outlawed", *International Affairs* (Moscow) (No. 8, 1971), p. 83 (discussing both UN General Assembly resolution 2645 (XXV), 1970, and The Hague Convention of December 1970); A. Makhovskii, "Zakhvat grazhdanskogo vozdushnogo sydna v svete mezhdunarodnogo prava", *Sovetskoe Gosudarstvo i Pravo* (No. 8, 1971), p. 59.

On 3 January 1973 the Soviet Union published a new law on criminal liability for the hijacking of aircraft (*Pravda* and *Izvestiya,* 4 January 1973). And see the discussion of the new law by V. Ivanov, in *Izvestiya,* 16 January 1973. The new Soviet law is discussed in greater detail in Chapter 3, *5, (b), infra.*

prehensive solution, and with the only area that seemed objectively suitable for a bilateral solution—the wave of hijackings from the United States to Cuba from the opening of the decade of the 1960s onwards—seemingly hampered, in terms of offering a formal legal solution, by the absence of formal diplomatic relations between the United States and Cuba over that same time period, the most directly available route to control of the proliferating nuisance of hijacking seemed to be recourse to multilateralism—the multilateral convention, and preferably a multilateral convention negotiated and drafted and adopted under the auspices of the international agency organised for, and having special competence in, the field of international commercial aviation—the International Civil Aviation Organization. And in terms of diplomatic and professional legal effort, the multilateral convention has been the instrument most utilised up to the present for purposes of attempting an international solution to the aerial hijacking problem.

Before going on to appraise the concrete record of achievement and the concrete record of failure by the multilateral treaty route, some observations should be made as to the general experience with multilateral treaties, in their immediate, post-World War II heyday, as an instrument for international legal problem-solving.

First, there will often be a very substantial time-lag between treaty-signing on the part of individual States, and the necessary legal follow-up by those same States in terms of treaty-ratification; and we can go beyond this by identifying an "attrition factor", in regard to all multilateral treaties, as between those who sign and eventually ratify on the one hand, and those who sign but never have any serious intention of ratifying in the first place.[5] Signature, coupled with a covert intention not to ratify subsequently, seems, in this regard, for some States, to be a rather less abrasive (though rather less courageous) way of opting out of an international law-making venture *via* the

5. See, in this regard, the study by O. Schachter, M. Nawaz, and J. Fried, *Toward Wider Acceptance of U.N. Treaties* (UNITAR (1971)), which, at pp. 24 *et seq.*, in a detailed analysis of statistical data regarding acceptance of UN treaties, offers striking lessons as to the over-all extent of acceptances of general multilateral treaties (ratifications, accessions, and successions), and also the over-all extent of treaty signatures that are *not* followed up by treaty ratifications.

treaty route.[6] To be sure, there are some other, more strictly technical, factors which also explain the widespread non-ratifications of multilateral treaties. But the existence of this phenomenon of the gap between signature and ratification of treaties seriously undermines the claims to a "World Community" action simply because a large number of countries have taken part in a diplomatic conference and have signed the document emerging at the end of it.

As a second general point, there seems to be something of an inverse relation between the number of States taking part in a multilateral convention, and the specificity and concreteness—or "bite"—of that convention. In other words, the greater the number of people who take part in the convention, the more likely it is that the convention will be vague and general or purely hortatory in its substantive contents, and lacking in specific remedies that are immediately operational in terms of actual problem-solving. That this should be so is not of course surprising: rather than run the risk of public failure involved in the break-up of a diplomatic conference without an agreed consensus document to produce at the end of it, the emphasis tends to be upon strictly verbal accommodations achieved through formulae expressed at such a very high level of generality and abstraction that they can mean all things to all men: an excellent example of this may be the United Nations General Assembly's resolution on Friendly Relations and Co-operation among States in accordance with the UN Charter, which was finally adopted in 1970 after seven years of arduous labours on the part of specialised UN Committees.

It is perhaps therefore not so surprising that the multilateral convention route to international legal problem-solving—and this as evidenced in the specific area of control of aerial hijacking,—so often ends up with legal pleonasms and the statement of the legally self-evident or obvious; or with a mere repetition of pre-existing (meaning here, pre-Convention) international law, and this even on the part of treaties that had, as their original design, to make new law, and not simply serve as "declaratory" or "restatement"-style treaties. There may also be one inherent, though certainly unintended defect of the treaty route to international legal problem-solving in the aerial hijac-

6. The relevant statistics as to treaty signatures and treaty ratifications in regard to each of the three multilateral conventions concerning the illegal diversion of aircraft—the Tokyo Convention of 1963, the Hague Convention of 1970, and the Montreal Convention of 1971—are given in the detailed discussion of each of these conventions, Chapter 3, *1, (a), (b),* and *(c), infra.*

king control area—namely the perverse tendency in many quarters to assume that, in making a treaty on a particular subject, that treaty automatically displaces the already existing customary international law in that subject area, and that even prior to ratification of the treaty; so that non-signatory or non-ratifying countries are, by their non-signature or non-ratification, automatically relieved from their obligation to adhere to the pre-existing customary international law. This is especially noticeable perhaps in regard to the first major attempt at international law-making in regard to aerial hijacking by the multilateral convention route; namely, the Tokyo Convention of 1963.

1. The Treaty Route: the Multilateral Convention

(a) The Tokyo Convention of 1963 (Convention on Offences and Certain Other Acts Committed On Board Aircraft)

The original purpose of the diplomatic negotiations which led up to the Tokyo Convention was to try to define the legal status of aircraft and to establish both judicial jurisdiction and also the applicable substantive law to govern alleged offences committed on board aircraft in flight; and even to establish the legal powers of the aircraft commander over the aircraft and its aircrew and passengers while in flight. These questions, while academically interesting and also generally important, had no particular element of urgency over a number of years, and so a series of meetings was held, with no particular pressures for quick solutions over the five-year period from 1958 to 1963. In origin, in any case, these discussions had absolutely nothing to do with aircraft hijacking, as such: it was not until 1962, at the ICAO Legal Committee meeting in Rome, that Venezuela and the United States suggested that the then proposed new Convention on the Legal Status of Aircraft should make specific reference to aircraft hijacking. The new proposals advanced in 1962 were to the effect that the State of first landing of a hijacked aircraft should restore control of the aircraft to its commander and take custody of the hijackers; that the State of first landing of the hijacked aircraft should permit the aircraft and its aircrew and passengers to continue on their journey as soon as practicable. These provisions with certain modifications were to become Article 11 of the Tokyo Convention of 1963.[7]

---

7. A. Lowenfeld, *Aviation Law, Cases and Materials* (1972), Ch. 7, s. 3. 3;

If we look at the substantive provisions of the Tokyo Convention, signed on 14 September 1963, the more long-range and prosaic (non-hijacking) elements in its historical origins become clear. But it does, in its general (non-hijacking) provisions, clearly recognise principles as to jurisdiction and control over aircraft which have important application to actual cases of hijacking too. The Convention recognises (in Article 3) the jurisdiction of the State of registration of the aircraft over offences and acts committed on board; and it also recognises (in Article 4) a criminal jurisdiction on the part of a State other than the State of registration of the aircraft among other things in respect to offences committed on board an aircraft that have effect on the territory of that State; and in respect to offences by or against a national or permanent resident of that State; and in respect to an offence against the security of that State. Articles 5 to 10 of the Tokyo Convention ("Powers of the Aircraft Commander") give to the aircraft commander substantial powers of control, including restraint, where he has—"reasonable grounds to believe that a person has committed, or is about to commit, on board the aircraft" (Article 6) —the offences or acts specified in the opening of the Convention; namely—

> "acts which, whether or not they are offences, may or do jeopardise the safety of the aircraft or of persons or property therein or which jeopardise good order and discipline on board" (Article 1).

The provisions of the Tokyo Convention that are deliberately and specifically oriented to the problem of aerial hijacking are contained in Article 11 ("Unlawful Seizure of Aircraft"):

> "Article 11. (1) When a person on board has unlawfully committed by force or threat thereof an act of interference, seizure, or other wrongful exercise of control of an aircraft in

---

G. F. FitzGerald, "Toward Legal Suppression of Acts against Civil Aviation", in *Air Hijacking: An International Perspective* (*International Conciliation,* (November 1971)), p. 47; Ryuichi Hirano, "Convention on Offences and Other Acts Committed on Board Aircraft of 1963", *Japanese Annual of International Law,* Vol. 8 (1964), p. 44. For detailed analysis and criticism of the Tokyo Convention provisions, and their comparison with the later, the Hague, Convention, see the comments of Professor J. H. W. Verzijl, *Annuaire de l'Institut de droit international,* Vol. 54, I ("Hijacking of Aircraft") (1971), pp. 520 *et seq.*

flight or when such an act is about to be committed, Contracting States shall take all appropriate measures to restore control of the aircraft to its lawful commander or to preserve his control of the aircraft.

(2) In the cases contemplated in the preceding paragraph, the Contracting State in which the aircraft lands shall permit its passengers and crew to continue their journey as soon as practicable and shall return the aircraft and its cargo to the persons lawfully entitled to possession."

This is what we meant, a little earlier, by referring to a tendency, in multilateral conventions, to render legal pleonasms—a statement of the already existing, pre-Convention, customary international law; and what, in terms of the subsequent State practice in regard to the Tokyo Convention, we meant also by saying that there seems to be a perverse tendency on the part of States that do not sign or do not ratify such a Convention to conclude that the adoption of such a Convention in effect displaces altogether the already-existing, pre-Convention, customary international law and automatically relieves those States, as non-signatories to the Convention, from any obligation to observe and respect that already-existing, pre-Convention, customary international law. As the *Institut de droit international* expressly recognised, at its 1971 reunion in Zagreb, not merely are the obligations that are reproduced in Article 11 of the Tokyo Convention of 1963 a matter of common humanity or ordinary decency on the part of nations;[8] but they are historically well rooted in the rules of classical, customary international law as to "Distress", establishing the obligation on the part of all States to render all possible aid and comfort to vessels undergoing shipwreck or otherwise in distress, and to do everything possible to speed them on their way to their original destination with their passengers and their crew and cargo, and this, seemingly, even in time of war between the involuntary host country and the country of the ship's flag.[9] Yet even since the Tokyo Convention restated these time-

8. Thus, the International Court of Justice in the *Corfu Channel Case (Merits)*, speaks of "elementary considerations of humanity, even more exacting in peace than in war". *International Court of Justice*, 1949, *Reports of Judgments*. Judgment of 9 April 1949, at p. 22. And see generally *Annuaire de l'Institut de droit international*, Vol. 54, I ("Hijacking of Aircraft") (1971), pp. 520 *et seq.* And see also O. J. Lissitzyn, "Hijacking, International Law, and Human Rights", in *Aerial Piracy and International Law* (E. McWhinney (Editor) (1971)).

9. For the classical international law base see, for example, H. Lauterpacht (Editor), *International Law. A Treatise*, Vol. I (8th edition, 1955), p. 504, note

honoured customary international law principles in multilateral treaty form, these very principles have been flagrantly ignored by certain countries in actual instances of aerial hijackings arising since the signing of the Tokyo Convention in 1963.[10]

1, p. 607; C. J. Colombos, *The International Law of the Sea* (4th revised edition, 1959), p. 289, p. 543; H. Krüger, "Seenot", in H. J. Schlochauer (Editor), *Wörterbuch des Völkerrechts,* Vol. 3 (1962), p. 237; W. Wengler, *Völkerrecht,* Vol. 2 (1964), pp. 1078, 1080, 1148; *Annuaire de l'Institut de droit international,* Vol. 17 (1898), p. 284. And see generally *Annuaire de l'Institut de droit international,* Vol. 54, I ("Hijacking of Aircraft") (1971), pp. 520 *et seq.*; *United States on behalf of Kate A. Hoff* v. *United Mexican States, General Claims Commission, Opinions* 174 (1929).

10. The Resolution of the *Institut de Droit International,* on "Unlawful Diversion of Aircraft", adopted at the Zagreb Session, on 3 September 1971, without dissenting vote, included the following declaratory principles restating already existing International Law obligations:

> "The Institute of International Law . . .
>
> II. Notes that, among others, the following rules of international law apply:
>
> . . . .
>
> 2. Under the general rules of international law which find particular expression in Articles 25 and 37 of the Chicago Convention of 1944, States are required to render assistance to aircraft in distress in their territory and to permit, subject to control by their own authorities, the owners of the aircraft or authorities of the States in which the aircraft is registered to provide such measures of assistance as may be necessitated by the circumstances . . .
>
> *Expresses the opinion that,* in consequence, States must take all appropriate measures to give effect to these principles, notably by taking action: . . .
>
> *(b)* in cases where an unlawfully diverted aircraft lands in their territory,
> — to restore control of the unlawfully diverted aircraft to its lawful commander or to preserve his control of the aircraft,
> — to permit the passengers and crew of the aircraft to continue their journey as soon as practicable,
> — to return the aircraft and its cargo to the persons lawfully entitled to possession,
> — to ensure the personal safety and human dignity of the passengers and crew until their journey can be continued."

Annuaire de l'Institut de droit international, Vol. 54 (1971).

The Chicago Convention of 1944 (Convention on International Civil Aviation), provides, in Article 25 (Aircraft in Distress): "Each contracting State undertakes to provide such measures of assistance to aircraft in distress in its territory as it may find practicable, and to permit, subject to control by its own authorities, the owners of the aircraft or authorities of the State in which the aircraft is registered to provide such measures of assistance at may be necessitated by the circumstances . . .".

Article 37 of the Chicago Convention (Adoption of international standards and procedures) requires States to collaborate in securing uniformity in regulations, standards, procedures, and organisation . . . "in all matters in which

Having said that the Tokyo Convention of 1963 restated, in treaty form, already-existing customary international law principles rather than itself breaking new ground in international law, we might have been expected to say that the Convention quickly achieved near universal approval and, more importantly, legal ratification. This was not to be the case! Although, in terms of Article 21 of the Convention, the Convention was to come into force 90 days after it should have been ratified by 12 of the original signatory States, it was not until the end of 1969—more than six years after the Convention's original signing—that the twelfth State, the United States, finally got around to ratifying it. (Canada, a State which has often expressed in public fine sentiments upon the principle of the "freedom of the air", did not ratify until *after* the Convention had already come into force, Canada being the thirteenth State to ratify.) I mention these facts only to signal the substantial element of political attrition that inevitably attends even perfectly self-evident and harmless treaties like the Tokyo Convention of 1963 that have no real teeth in them. On the record, even those States most publicly committed to the "Rule of Law" in international law, can be found among the delinquents in regard to the prompt follow-up of their international law obligations.[11]

(b) *The Hague Convention of 1970* (Convention for the Suppression of Unlawful Seizure of Aircraft)

The Hague Convention of 1970 arose for the two essential reasons:

---

such uniformity will facilitate and improve air navigation", and to this end charges ICAO with adopting and amending international standards and recommended practices and procedures dealing with: ... "(k) Aircraft in distress and investigation of accidents; and such other matters concerned with the safety, regularity, and efficiency of air navigation as may from time to time appear appropriate."

11. The Tokyo Convention was signed at Tokyo on 14 September 1963, and formally entered in force, in accordance with Article 21 (1) of the Convention, on 4 December 1969. The first 12 States to ratify the Tokyo Convention and to make it law, were, for the most part, major airline States with a proven record of observance of the provisions of the Chicago Convention of 1944 and of respect for the principle of the "freedom of the air"; and, in particular, none of the more notorious "delinquent" States was included in the list: Republic of China, Denmark, Italy, Mexico, Niger, Norway, Philippines, Portugal, Sweden, United Kingdom, United States, Upper Volta. According to the latest statistics furnished by ICAO on 19 April 1973, up to that date 42 countries had signed the Tokyo Convention, and 63 countries had ratified or else acceded to the Convention.

first, the expansion of the dimensions of the aerial hijacking problem throughout the 1960s (with the quietus to the Cold War, East-West, military espionage or refugee hijackings, as the Soviet-Western *détente* consolidated) from an essentially limited, US-Cuban, regional, inter-American or Caribbean, "nuisance" to a more genuinely world-wide problem affecting equally a number of countries with differing politi-cal-ideological bases; and second, the demonstrated inadequacy of the essentially hortatory, admonitory, anti-hijacking provisions contained in the Tokyo Convention of 1963. For the Tokyo Convention, and especially its Article 11, as we have noted, really did no more than re-state already existing customary international law obligations, without troubling to take the extra step of giving them some teeth by providing effective sanctions for their enforcement. In fairness to the drafters of the Tokyo Convention, of course, it must be remembered that, in its immediate historical origins, that Convention was not an anti-hijacking treaty, and that, as a whole, it focusses only incidentally on the hijacking problem.

As it happened, the preparatory diplomatic and drafting discussions to the Hague Convention focussed upon a solution originally raised by the United States at the 1962, Rome meeting of the ICAO Legal Committee that preceded the Tokyo Convention of 1963—namely the question of the extradition or punishment of a hijacker, in accordance with their own laws on the part of the State or States to which the hijacker might illegally divert the aircraft—a question, however, that was never really pressed at Rome in 1962 since generally considered, at the time, as being premature or even an over-reaction to the hijacking problem. This, of course, is the principle *aut dedere aut punire,* to which reference will be made later.

The formal preparations for the Hague Convention began in 1968 with a request by the ICAO Assembly that the ICAO Council study the problem of aerial hijacking as soon as possible, in view of the fact that Article 11 of the Tokyo Convention clearly did not provide a complete remedy;[12] and the ICAO Council immediately referred the

12. See generally A. Lowenfeld, *op. cit.* (1972), Ch. 7, s. 3. 5; G. F. Fitz-Gerald, *International Conciliation* (November 1971), p. 51; J. Ragski, "Konwencga haska o zwalczanin bezprawnego zawladniecia statkami powietrznymi", *Panstwo i Prawo* (1971), p. 708; A. Crivellaro, "Il progetto di Convenzione dell'O.A.C.I. relativo alla cattura illecita di aeromobili", *Giurisprudenza italiana* (1971), p. 3; Verzijl, *op. cit., supra,* footnote 7.

matter to the Legal Committee which produced a draft treaty that was ultimately adopted on 16 December 1970, at a diplomatic conference at which 77 member-States of ICAO were represented, including the USSR which had just joined ICAO. The convention itself was approved at the diplomatic conference by a vote of 74 to 0, with Algeria (and also Chile) abstaining. Cuba was not represented at the conference. No less that 50 of the States represented at the diplomatic conference signed the convention at the conclusion of the conference.

The Hague Convention opens by a definition of the offence of unlawful seizure of aircraft:

> "Article 1.
>
> Any person who on board an aircraft in flight:
>
> *(a)* unlawfully, by force or threat thereof, or by any other form of intimidation, seizes, or exercises control of, that aircraft, or attempts to perform any such act, or
>
> *(b)* is an accomplice of a person who performs or attempts to perform any such act
>
> commits an offence."

Under Article 2 of the Convention, each contracting State is to make the offence—"punishable by severe penalties". The Convention signally fails, however, to specify minimum penalties on the part of contracting States—the abandonment of this objective being one of the notable concessions that the proponents of strong action against hijacking were forced to make in pursuit of the elusive goal of a unanimous vote in favour of the Convention as a whole.

Each contracting State is also obligated, under Article 4 of the Convention, to take steps to establish its legal jurisdiction over unlawful seizures of aircraft and any other act of violence against passengers or crew committed in connection with the hijacking—when the offence is committed on board an aircraft registered in that State; or when the hijacked aircraft lands in that State with the hijacker still on board. This is a step forward, of course, though it is certainly not the same thing as universality of jurisdiction, thought by the proponents of strong action against hijacking to be necessary to assure an effective control of the problem, on the principle of an international "hue and cry" against the criminal hijacker on the part of all States having some point of contact with the actual problem-situation involved,—either because they are the State of registry of the hijacked aircraft; or the

State in whose airspace the hijacking is committed; or the State in which the hijacked aircraft lands; or the State of nationality of the hijacker or any of his accomplices, or of the pilot or any member of the aircrew, or of any one or more of the passengers.

Under Article 6 of the Convention, each contracting State is required to take the hijacker into custody for purposes of criminal or extradition proceedings, and to notify interested States to that effect. Under Article 7, the State in whose territory the hijacker is found, if it does not extradite him, is obliged—

> "without exception whatsoever and whether or not the offence was committed in its territory, to submit the case to its competent authorities for the purpose of prosecution.
>
> Those authorities shall take their decision in the same manner as in the case of any ordinary offence of a serious nature under the law of that State."

It is Article 7 which seeks to render into treaty form the obligation *aut dedere, aut punire* in the case of a hijacker. It is not of course fool-proof in terms of ensuring that the hijacker will actually be punished. The obligation of the contracting State, under the treaty, ceases with the submitting of the case to its own criminal prosecution department; and the follow-up there necessarily rests upon the competence and the diligence,—and the good faith—of those national civil servants, and their freedom or otherwise from their own government's direction and control in the matter.

Article 8 of the Convention attempts to deal with the difficult issue of extradition, raised by the establishment of the alternative obligation to extradite, if the State in which the hijacker is found should decide not to refer the hijacker to its criminal authorities for prosecution within that State. The Hague Convention could clearly not constitute, in itself, a comprehensive code on extradition in regard to hijackers, in replacement for the plethora of bilateral extradition treaties of a general nature already in existence between so many States. What Article 8 does is to declare that hijacking is to be—"deemed to be included as an extraditable offence" in any extradition treaty existing between contracting States; and that it is to be expressly included as an extraditable offence in any new extradition treaty between contracting States (Article 8 (1)). Where no extradition treaty is in effect between two contracting States, then, according to Article 8 (2), any one of the contracting States may, at its option, consider the Hague Convention as the legal basis for extradition in response to a request from the other State. Article 8 (2) is, in this regard, facultative or permissive, but in no sense obligatory, and it is, clearly, another political compromise between the "Hawks" and the "Doves" at the diplomatic conference at The Hague, having the result of drawing some more of the teeth from the potential community controls over hijacking, in deference once again to the elusive quest for a unanimous vote for adoption of the Convention.

Finally, Article 9 of the Hague Convention restates, with some minor changes, that basic international law obligation to an aircraft and its passengers and crew in distress,—which was restated from already-existing customary international law and which, under Article 11 of the Tokyo Convention of 1963, was re-affirmed once more as an obligation of all contracting States under the Convention in the case of a hijacking of aircraft. The new Article 9 (2) of the Hague Convention requires contracting States to—"*facilitate* the continuation of the journey of the passengers and crew as soon as practicable"; whereas Article 11 (2) of the Tokyo Convention, more unequivocally perhaps, required contracting States to "permit [the] passengers and crew to continue their journey as soon as practicable".

On the other hand, the new Article 9 (2) of the Hague Convention perhaps firms up the old Article 11 (2) of the Tokyo Convention by then going on to require contracting States "*without delay* to return the aircraft and its cargo to the persons lawfully entitled to possession"; where, by contrast, the old Article 11 (2) of the Tokyo Convention simply imposed the same obligation without making any specification as to the timing.

Article 12 (1) of the Hague Convention provides for negotiation, and then, failing that, arbitration, in the event of a dispute between two or more contracting States as to the Convention; and, after that, for reference of the dispute, on the motion of any one of the parties, to the International Court of Justice. But Article 12 (2) of the Convention expressly allows any State, at the time of its signature, ratification or accession to the Convention, to declare itself as not bound by this provision—an "opting out" clause as to judicial settlement of disputes that was introduced on the direct initiative of the Soviet Union, which has, since that time, expressly taken advantage of the exemption in its instrument of ratification of the Hague Convention.

With the experience of the extreme delays in ratification, and consequent coming into force, of the Tokyo Convention of 1963, the drafts of the Hague Convention were themselves modest as to the minimum number of ratifications necessary to bring the Convention into legal effect: Article 13 (3) of the Convention stipulated that it is to enter into force 30 days after ratification by *ten* States signatory to the Convention.[13]

(c) *The Montreal Convention of 1971* (Convention for the Suppression of Unlawful Acts Against the Safety of Civil Aviation)

The Montreal Convention, signed on 23 September 1971, is directed to the prevention and discouragement of sabotage and acts of violence generally—other than hijacking and acts of unlawful seizure—directed against aircraft, but also against civil aviation in general. It was intended as a supplement to the more specific (hijacking) prohibitions and protective controls contained in the Hague Convention, largely because, as a result in part of an increasing success in advance detection and prevention of aerial hijacking, through legal but also direct administrative and police measures, the criminal elements who had originally chosen hijacking as a spectacular and easily engineered method of vindicating their claims, turned to other methods which, if less effective perhaps, were more difficult to apprehend or counter in advance on the part of law-enforcement authorities. These acts of sabotage and violence (other than hijacking) were normally, though not exclusively, mounted by the same political forces that turned to hijacking as a form of "irregular" ("privileged") combatancy, to achieve political objectives that seemed to them not otherwise or as readily realisable under the normal international machinery processes for fundamental political or legal change. Of this specialised class of international criminal activity, then, the "Cold War" and also the "lunatic fringe" categories of hijackers have invariably not been a part, nor, for that matter, the "hijackers for gain" ("air bandits"); though there have been some isolated cases of apparently mentally unbalanced persons telephoning threats of aircraft sabotage to airline companies, and also cases of threats of physical destruction of aircraft made with a view to financial extortion against airline companies.

13. The Hague Convention was signed at The Hague on 16 December 1970, and entered into force, in accordance with Article 13 (3) of the Convention, on 14 October 1971. According to the latest statistics furnished by ICAO on 19 April 1973, up to that date 81 countries had signed the Hague Convention, and 54 countries had ratified or else acceded to the Convention.

By and large, however, this class of activity is an increasingly important alternative or secondary line of action for those international terrorist groups who have, in the past, mounted the major Middle East aerial hijackings. Although this activity does not fall within the strict definition of the diversion of aircraft in flight and is, therefore, also beyond the scope of the present lectures as strictly defined, the same basic legal policies are involved, and the same underlying conflicting social interests, as in the case of the international terrorist hijackings. And so we will make a brief *résumé* of the objectives and provisions of the Montreal Convention of 1971, in order to allow of the widest possible frame of reference for our identification and analysis of the alternative policy constructs, and also the alternative solutions flowing from them, for that most difficult of all categories of hijacking to control effectively at the international level—namely those hijackings raising basic issues of political-ideological conflict between States in terms of the ultimate motives for their being mounted and also the specific objectives to which they are directed.

The Montreal Convention of 1971,—or the Sabotage Convention, as it is sometimes called—follows the general plan of the Hague Convention of 1970 [14] with the attempt to create widespread jurisdiction over offences specified in the Convention and also with the imposition of the requirement of either extradition or prosecution of the criminal offenders on the part of contracting States.

The offence of Unlawful Acts against the Safety of Civil Aviation is defined in the opening provisions of the Montreal Convention—

> "Article 1. 1. Any person commits an offence if he unlawfully and intentionally:
>
> *(a)* performs an act of violence against a person on board an aircraft in flight if that act is likely to endanger the safety of that aircraft; or
>
> *(b)* destroys an aircraft in service or causes damage to such an aircraft which renders it incapable of flight or which is likely to endanger its safety in flight; or
>
> *(c)* places or causes to be placed on an aircraft in service, by any means whatsoever, a device or substance which is likely

14. See generally A. Lowenfeld, *op. cit.* (1972), Ch. 7, s. 3. 8; G. F. Fitz-Gerald, *International Conciliation* (November 1971), p. 66.

to destroy that aircraft, or to cause damage to it which renders it incapable of flight, or to cause damage to it which is likely to endanger its safety in flight; or

(d) destroys or damages air navigation facilities or interferes with their operation, if any such act is likely to endanger the safety of aircraft in flight; or

(e) communicates information which he knows to be false, thereby endangering the safety of an aircraft in flight."

Article 1 (2) of the Convention goes on to penalise the *attempt* to commit any of these offences, and also punishes accomplices of persons committing or attempting to commit the offences.

Article 5 (1) of the Convention obligates every contracting State to establish its jurisdiction—where the offence is committed in its territory; against or on board an aircraft registered in that State; when the aircraft on board which the offence is committed lands in its territory with the alleged offender still on board. Each contracting State is required, beyond this, to establish its jurisdiction in cases defined in Article 1 where the offender is present in its territory and it does not extradite him pursuant to the Convention (Article 5 (2)).

Under Article 7, a contracting State in which the offender is found, if it does not extradite him, is obliged,—"without exception whatsoever and whether or not the offence was committed in its territory, to submit the case to its competent authorities for the purpose of prosecution".

Article 8 of the Montreal Convention has the same basic provisions as included in the Hague Convention of 1970, as to treating offences under the Convention as extraditable offences in any extradition treaty between contracting States, either existing treaties or those to be included in the future; and it also, as in the case of the Hague Convention, gives contracting States the option of considering the Convention as the legal basis for extradition, in the case of requests for extradition from other contracting States with which it has no extradition treaty.

Article 14 of the Montreal Convention follows the Hague Convention as to dispute settlement, including arbitration and possible reference to the International Court of Justice, with the right of any contracting State, in making its ratification of the Convention, to opt out altogether as to these provisions.

In terms of Article 15, the Montreal Convention is, on the lines of the Hague Convention, to enter into force 30 days after ratification by *ten* States signatory to the Convention.[15]

(d) *Enforcement of the Tokyo, the Hague, and the Montreal Conventions. Draft Proposals for a Convention on Sanctions*

If the Tokyo Convention of 1963 can fairly be described as purely hortatory in practical significance, the two later Conventions of The Hague and Montreal do attempt to face up to the problem of applying sanctions to the individual hijacker or aircraft saboteur, by requiring contracting States either to extradite the offender when they find him within their territory, or themselves to move to punish the offender. But there are several important gaps in the coverage thereby provided. First, the host State that receives the hijacker or saboteur is, in the event that it does not extradite him, bound under the Hague and Montreal Conventions only to submit his case to its competent authorities for the purpose of prosecution. But there is no guarantee that prosecution will in fact follow; and also no provision for any follow-up, under the two Conventions, as to the degree of diligence or good faith exercised by the host State in actually ensuring that there will be prosecution and subsequent punishment of the offender. Second, there is no provision, under the Hague and Montreal Conventions, as to possible sanctions against a contracting State that wilfully or negligently fails to honour its obligation, under the Conventions, either to extradite or to prosecute.

The United States has pressed most vigorously for a sanctions plan to be applied against delinquent States that fail to honour their obligations under these Conventions. The key to the United States plan has been the proposal for collective action, by the signatories to the Conventions, to suspend airline services (involving flights in and out of the countries concerned) with those countries refusing to honour the obligation either to extradite or to punish aerial hijackers or aircraft saboteurs generally. In the ICAO Council reunion in the Autumn of 1970, meeting in the immediate aftermath of the mass international

---

15. The Montreal Convention was signed at Montreal on 23 September 1971, and entered into force, in accordance with Article 15 of the Convention, on 26 January 1973. According to the latest statistics furnished by ICAO on 19 April 1973, up to that date 63 countries had signed the Montreal Convention, and 26 countries had ratified or else acceded to the Convention.

terrorist hijackings to the Jordanian desert, the United States put forward a concrete sanctions plan, built around the idea of an aerial blockade against a delinquent State that detains a hijacked aircraft and its passengers and aircrew within its territory for international blackmail purposes, or that harbours or otherwise gives protection within its territory to a criminal hijacker. The United States Draft Convention on Sanctions (a Convention regarding the Safety and Security of International Civil Air Transport Services) was presented as a Working Paper and circulated by the ICAO Legal Committee in October 1970.[16]

The United States Draft Convention opens with a very broad definition of the range of "interested States" competent to invoke sanctions action in terms of the Draft Convention (Article 1). In the case of unlawful seizure (hijacking), it is to be the State of registration of the aircraft, and any State whose nationals are on board the aircraft; and in the case of unlawful interference (sabotage), it is to be, in addition to these States, the State within whose jurisdiction such unlawful interference took place. Under Article 2, whenever any interested State has reason to believe that a hijacking has occurred, and that the hijacked aircraft, its passengers or crew are being detained, —contrary to Article 11 of the Tokyo Convention of 1963—within the territory of another State for international blackmail purposes, it may put in motion the sanctions-applying procedures, involving a meeting and then majority vote of all "interested States" together with any other States operating civil air services to or from the alleged detaining State. Under Article 3, similar procedures may be applied on the initiative of any "interested State", where it has reason to believe that another State is harbouring a person who has either committed a hijacking or else committed an act of unlawful interference (sabotage) resulting in damage to the aircraft or death or physical injury to a passenger or aircrew member: this Article is predicated upon a failure of the second State to take the criminal delinquent into immediate custody and thereafter to extradite or prosecute such person. In the event of a finding of default in its international obligations against any State in pursuance of Article 2 or Article 3, the stage is then set for follow-up action—specifically, joint action to suspend all

16. ICAO Legal Committee. Working Paper presented by the United States delegation. Draft Convention on Sanctions. (A Convention regarding the Safety and Security of International Civil Air Transport Services.) (LC/Working Draft No. 776, 9 October 1970.)

civil air services directly or indirectly to and from the State determined to be in default, plus any other measures intended to assure the safety and security of international civil air service to and from the State determined to be in default (Article 4). Article 7 of the US Draft Convention, operating as a declaratory article, stipulated that suspension of authority for any carrier to operate international civil air transport services, pursuant to a joint action decision under Article 4, should be considered consistent with the obligations of States under the Chicago Convention of 1944, and should not be considered inconsistent with any bilateral air transport agreement existing between States parties to the Chicago Convention: contracting States under the US Draft Convention were also, in terms of Article 7, to undertake not to include any provisions inconsistent with the Draft Convention in any bilateral air transport agreement to be concluded by them.

As an international law agreement the US Draft Convention really did seem to have some teeth in it; for it would have, symbolically but also effectively, sent any delinquent State into "Coventry" within the "special legal community" of the air, by isolating that delinquent State from the range of operation of international civil air services, at least on the part of all other "law-abiding" States (meaning, here, all those States choosing to honour the provisions of the Draft Convention, whether as signatories to the Draft Convention, or else as non-signatories). Understandably perhaps because of the "teeth" that it did have in it, in comparison to other Conventions already existing in the same field, the US Draft Convention encountered immediate, and eminently predictable, difficulties within the ICAO Council and the ICAO Legal Committee, these difficulties manifesting themselves especially in parliamentary-style proceduralisms and other obstructions placed in the way of the Draft Convention in the form of delaying tactics.

An originally innocuous, US-introduced resolution, calling only for *consultations*—"with a view to deciding what joint action should be undertaken, in accordance with international law, without excluding measures such as the suspension of international civil air transport services"—was adopted by the ICAO Council on 1 October 1970, by a vote of 14 to 3, with 10 abstentions.[17]

17. ICAO. Council Guidelines for Eighteenth Session of ICAO Legal Committee. First Resolution adopted by the Council on 1 October 1970 (LXXI-6) (LC/SC CR-Report, Appendix C).

It was in response to this resolution and to the direction, contained at the end of the resolution, to the ICAO Legal Committee to consider during its forthcoming Eighteenth Session an international convention or other international instruments to give effect to the principle of the resolution, that the United States had first introduced its Draft Convention on Sanctions, circulated in the ICAO Legal Committee as a Working Paper on 9 October 1970.

The US Draft was later modified in certain respects and resubmitted as a joint US-Canadian Draft,[18] to a special ICAO Legal Committee sub-committee which met in April 1971. This sub-committee completed about one-half of its work at the April 1971 meeting, and at its concluding session approved an interim report recommending that the sub-committee meet again "as soon as possible in order to complete its work". Subsequently, the ICAO Council set aside the last two weeks of February of 1972 for further sub-committee study of the Draft Convention. However, the Eighteenth ICAO Assembly, meeting in Vienna in June of 1971, voted to move consideration of this proposal from the "active" to the "inactive" part of the work programme of the Legal Committee. This meant that until further action should be taken by the ICAO Council or the ICAO Assembly directing the work to be completed, neither the ICAO Legal Committee nor its legal sub-committee would consider the subject further. In fact, the meeting of the legal sub-committee that had earlier been scheduled for the last two weeks of February 1972, to consider the matter, was promptly assigned a quite different subject for its agenda.

The matter thus drifted along, in limbo, until the Summer of 1972, without any concrete action resulting, until finally another rash of hijackings around that time induced the International Federation of Airline Pilots Associations, as a measure of self-help in default of any positive response by the *official* legal community of the Air—ICAO, and indeed the United Nations Security Council and General Assembly—to set a global, 24-hour strike of airline pilots, involving a shut-down of world air services, for 19 June 1972.[19] At this sudden threat of direct action, ICAO at long last began to move again; and on 19 June 1972, the ICAO Council adopted a Special Resolution [20]

18. LC/SC CR-Report, Appendix D.

19. *New York Times,* 11 June 1972; *ibid.,* 17 June 1972. *Le Devoir* (Montreal), 17 June 1972.

20. ICAO. Resolution adopted by the ICAO Council, 19 June 1972. Reproduced in *International Legal Materials,* Vol. 9 (July 1972), at p. 897.

which, after the usual recitals of past resolutions of the ICAO Assembly and of the UN General Assembly and Security Council, directed the ICAO Legal Committee to convene immediately a special subcommittee to work on the preparation of an international convention establishing multi-national procedures, within the general ICAO framework, for enforcement of the three anti-air-piracy conventions already adopted—the Tokyo Convention of 1963, the Hague Convention of 1970, and the Montreal Convention of 1971.[21]

The ICAO Legal Committee's sub-committee met in Washington at the beginning of September 1972, and it immediately had as its main agenda item a newly updated version of the original United States Draft Convention on Sanctions that had been presented by the United States delegation as a Working Paper to the ICAO Legal Committee on 9 October 1970.[22] There was immediate political sparring in the ICAO legal sub-committee meeting in Washington, one of the first moves of the United States being to compel a vote on whether to hold the sessions in public.[23] The United States pressed for the session to be held in public in order to secure the maximum possible pressure of public opinion upon the individual national delegates. As it was, the motion to hold the sessions in public was adopted by nine votes to five, with a strange alliance of the Soviet Union, the United Arab Republic, Chile, France, and Great Britain voting against holding the meetings in public.[24] When the updated US Sanctions proposals were presented, they involved, once again, collective sanctions against individual countries failing to comply with the provisions of the three main Conventions, these sanctions looking, in particular, to the cutting off of civil air service to the delinquent countries and to similar measures. These sanction proposals were promptly opposed by France, Great Britain and the Soviet Union, although for somewhat different reasons in each case.

The meeting in Washington in September 1972 started out with a very strong statement by the United States Secretary of Transportation, Mr. Volpe, to the effect that just as direct action had proved the only

21. The ICAO Council Resolution of 19 June 1972, was adopted by a vote of 17 to 1 (United Arab Republic), with 7 abstentions (Congo, India, Indonesia, Nigeria, Tunisia, Uganda and the Soviet Union). *International Legal Materials,* Vol. 9 (July 1972), at p. 897.

22. *New York Times,* 2 September 1972.

23. *Ibid.,* 5 September 1972.

24. *Ibid.*

solution to the problem of piracy on the high seas by denying havens to the original sea pirates, so the only effective control of aerial piracy was similar direct action.[25] The United States measures (which were, as already noted, co-sponsored by Canada at this stage), were soon seen to be doomed to failure, facing as they did almost certain defeat by a sort of "un-Holy Alliance" of France, Great Britain, the Soviet Union and the United Arab Republic. The United States therefore withdrew its Draft Convention and acquiesced reluctantly in a French proposal to start writing a new treaty from scratch.[26]

Now it isn't too difficult to speculate as to the reasons for the differences in national attitudes, leading to differences in political positions taken, in the ICAO Legal Committee sub-committee meeting in Washington. It was speculated in the public press, at the time, for example, that the British were very worried about continuity of their aerial routes through the Middle East; and that the British also didn't want to take any action that might possibly embarrass them in their dealings with those Arab States of the Middle East in which they still had extensive oil interests.[27] It was also said in the public press that the French, for their part, felt that they might be put in the invidious position, if the US-Canadian sanctions proposals were adopted, of having to take action against Algeria which had been a former member of the French Empire and had only recently gained its independence from France; and that, in consequence, the French felt that their best possible course of action at this stage was to avoid any action at all.[28] On the other hand, the Soviet Union was caught in the difficult situation of needing to balance itself between the demands of the Afro-Asian countries who, as a general rule, resisted any anti-air piracy measures with teeth in them, and the Soviet Union's own new awareness, in the light of the recent wave of hijacking incidents within the Soviet Union itself, of the genuine importance of the classical international law principle of the freedom of the air. The way out of this philosopher's dilemma, for the Soviet Union, was to announce its acceptance of the idea of sanctions against aerial hijackers and saboteurs, as such; but to insist, on an institutional-machinery basis, that any such sanctions action could only be constitutionally possible when taken through

25. *New York Times,* 5 September 1972.
26. *Ibid.,* 6 September 1972.
27. *Ibid.,* 6 September 1972; *ibid.,* 10 September 1972.
28. *Ibid.,* 5, 6, 7, 10 September 1972; *The Sunday Times* (London), 3 September 1972.

the ultimate United Nations organ responsible for international security,—meaning, here, the UN Security Council, in which of course, as a Permanent Member, the Soviet Union had a veto power on any action.[29] And so, in the end result, the Soviet Union supported the British and the French and voted against the American-Canadian joint proposals.

These different national oppositions to the American-Canadian proposals were presented with varying degrees of political skill or verbal sophistication. The British compromise proposal, offered instead of the American-Canadian Draft Convention, was to create a fact-finding board of States so as to establish whether there was in fact any threat to air safety; but the British didn't really go on to suggest any further steps. And, of course, one of the more general, and technically-based, objections to the US-Canadian proposals was that they seemed to require the application of sanctions even against non-signatory countries to the three Conventions; and it was objected that that would be too novel and dramatic a step in international law terms. In the result, in any case, the American-Canadian proposals were doomed, and they were therefore withdrawn; and so one had *tabula rasa* again while the British and the French proposals were brought forth. This was enough for the *New York Times,* in an Editorial on 7 September 1972, to accuse the ICAO Legal Committee sub-committee of "fuzzy governmental thinking" and to speak very strongly and critically of Soviet and French "foot-dragging".[30] It should be added, by the way, that the Soviet Union,—while objecting strenuously to any requirement of collective action against individual countries unless such action be taken through the UN Security Council,—was at the same time asking for *mandatory* extradition of *all* aircraft hijackers,[31] an approach that, for a combination of reasons, none of the other major countries had seemed prepared to take, up to the present time.

So for all of these reasons the 15-nation Washington Conference of the ICAO Legal Committee sub-committee ended without a treaty, and with no decision; and for this non-event it was very strongly criticised by the Airline Pilots Associations and others.[32]

The action now shifted to the ICAO Legal Committee proper, which

29. *New York Times,* 5, 6, 7, 10 September 1972.
30. Editorial, "Hijacking Uncurbed", *New York Times,* 7 September 1972.
31. *New York Times,* 6 September 1972.
32. *Ibid.,* 16 September 1972.

met in January 1973, and had before it the achievements, or non-achievements, of the Washington Legal Committee sub-committee conference. Various proposals now came forward that had been advanced in preliminary form in Washington after the withdrawal of the American-Canadian Draft Convention. What the ICAO Legal Committee then did was to adopt, on 27 January 1973, a resolution calling, in effect, for two more meetings:[33] the first one to be an extraordinary session of the ICAO Assembly (that is, the Assembly of the whole 124 members of ICAO); and the second one to be a further diplomatic conference. The stated object of each of these two proposed, further gatherings was to get adoption of multilateral agreements relating to suppression of acts of hijacking and possibly also other unlawful acts of interference (sabotage).[34]

For the proposed extraordinary session of the ICAO Assembly, the Legal Committee recommended, on a joint Austrian-West German motion, that the following two proposals be considered: the first a proposal by France that would, in effect, incorporate into the Chicago Convention of 1944 the provisions of the Hague Convention of 1970 for the suppression of hijacking of aircraft.[35] The net effect of this would be that failure of any member State of ICAO to ratify the proposed amendment of the Chicago Convention, after that amendment had entered into force (that is to say, the amendment incorporating into the Chicago Convention the Hague Convention provisions), would result in the expulsion of the defaulting State from ICAO. You can see that this particular French-sponsored proposal is oriented to action within the political-institutional projection of the "special legal community" of the air—the international, inter-governmental "air club", ICAO, established in terms of the Chicago Convention of 1944.

---

33. The ICAO Legal Committee's Resolution of 27 January 1973, was adopted by a vote of 38 to 8, with 11 abstentions, *New York Times,* 28 January 1973; *International Legal Materials,* Vol. 12 (March 1973), p. 377; *United Nations, Press Section,* Press Release WS/592, 2 February 1973; *United Nations Law Reports,* Vol. 7, No. 6 (1 February 1973), p. 27.

34. In accordance with the Legal Committee's recommendation, the ICAO Council decided on 7 March 1973, to convene an extraordinary session of the ICAO Assembly, and a diplomatic conference, in Rome from 28 August to 21 September 1973, and to submit the proposals to these two bodies. *International Legal Materials,* Vol. 12 (March 1973), p. 377.

35. French draft amendment to the Chicago Convention. Note presented by the French Government, ICAO Legal Committee—20th Session (Special) (Montreal, 9-30 January 1973), LC/Working Draft No. 821, 15 December 1972. *International Legal Materials,* Vol. 12 (March 1973), pp. 378 *et seq.*

A second Austrian-West German suggestion as to matters to be submitted to the poposed extraordinary session of the ICAO Assembly was an originally Great Britain-Switzerland, jointly-sponsored amendment to the Chicago Convention of 1944. This Great Britain-Switzerland amendment [36] was designed to oblige a State in whose territory an alleged offender was present, to take measures for the detention of that offender and for ensuring either his prosecution or his extradition; and further, to require the State of landing to facilitate the continuation of the journey of the passengers, crew, and aircraft; with the penalty, in a case where the ICAO Council should decide that the State concerned hadn't complied with those provisions, that other contracting States of ICAO would not allow the operation of an airline of the defaulting State through their territories.

The second main proposal of the ICAO Legal Committee at its meeting in January 1973, and as expressed in its resolution of 27 January 1973, was, as we have mentioned, the convening of a special diplomatic conference; and this was also to have two matters submitted to it. The first matter was a sort of Scandinavian suggestion (Denmark, Finland, Norway, and Sweden),[37] and it was a proposal for another new convention which would provide, in a case of hijacking or unlawful interference, for an inquiry into the facts (fact-finding) by the ICAO Council or a Commission of Experts appointed by it; with any subsequent action to include a recommendation made by the ICAO Council to a State in default because of its failure to take measures against alleged offenders. The second matter to be submitted to the special diplomatic conference was one put forward by the Soviet Union,[38] providing for Protocols to the Hague and Montreal Conventions, these Protocols obliging States parties to those Conventions to extradite an alleged offender to the State of registry of the hijacked or sabotaged aircraft on receipt of request from that State, except

---

36. Swiss-United Kingdom draft amendments to the Chicago Convention, LC/Working Draft No. 829, and Addenda, 17 January 1973, *International Legal Materials,* Vol. 12 (March 1973), pp. 383 *et seq.*

37. The Nordic draft. Proposal by the Delegations of Denmark, Finland, Norway and Sweden, LC/Working Draft No. 831, *Revised,* 24 January 1973. *International Legal Materials,* Vol. 12 (March 1973), pp. 387 *et seq.*

38. The USSR draft protocol. Draft protocol to the Convention for the Suppression of Unlawful Seizure of Aircraft signed at The Hague on 16 December 1970. LC/Working Draft No. 826, 9 January 1973, *International Legal Materials,* Vol. 12 (March 1973), pp. 390-391.

where the offender was a national of the State receiving such a request for extradition.

To re-capitulate, the 27 January 1973 resolution of the ICAO Legal Committee thus provides for the convening of two more conferences —one an ICAO Assembly extraordinary session, and the second a Diplomatic Conference—with more proposals to consider. In the debate in the ICAO Legal Committee, the US-Canadian proposals had been effectively beaten by a vote of 30 to 14, with 5 abstentions, when the ICAO Legal Committee approved a Swedish proposal to debate the "basic principle" of sanctions (rather than sanctions themselves);[39] and this was the strategy that enforced indefinite postponement of the discussion of the US-Canadian Draft Convention. It is clear that though the ICAO Legal Committee's final decision is to continue discussions, it means, inevitably, another major time-lag before any concrete measures can emerge.

Some interesting and (in the ICAO context) new thoughts did emerge from the otherwise abortive ICAO Legal Committee meeting of January 1973: for example, the Senegal delegate stated that since studies showed that, of 300 hijacking cases, 64 per cent. were "due to political forces", it appeared that it might be tactically fruitful, within ICAO, to try to distinguish between "political" and "non-political" motivations for hijackings.[40] For there was the clear implication that if, in the contemporary climate of ICAO, one could hardly realistically expect action on the two-thirds "political" hijacking cases, one could at least solve the one-third, "non-politically-motivated" hijackings.

But all this sustained non-action on the part of ICAO's Legal Committee provoked widespread public criticism. *Le Devoir* of Montreal, the leading (French-language) Canadian daily, published at the seat of ICAO itself, attacked the ICAO meeting as an "abdication of responsibility" in its indefinite shelving of the US-Canadian sanctions proposals;[41] and *Le Devoir* went on to declare, categorically, that ICAO had once again accomplished nothing.[42] The *New York Times* described the ICAO Legal Committee meeting as a "loaded meeting"; and it ended with the comment,—"If the Montreal meeting can do no

39. *New York Times,* 14 January 1973.
40. *Ibid.*
41. *Le Devoir* (Montreal), 19 January 1973.
42. "La piraterie aérienne, L'OACI n'a encore rien accompli", *Le Devoir* (Montreal), 24 January 1973.

better than this, it might as well give up. An enforcement treaty that provides no clear enforcement measures will add nothing significant to the toothless agreements already on the books." [43]

Perhaps the most telling comment on the obvious failure of the 63-nation ICAO Legal Committee, was the wry comment of the delegate from Qatar, to the effect that ICAO shouldn't be "like a fashion house such as Dior or St. Laurent"—turning out new-model treaties every year.[44]

(e) *Critique of the basic, sanctions-based approach to enforcement of the Tokyo, the Hague, and the Montreal Conventions*

The spearhead of the intellectual criticisms of the US-Canadian Draft Convention on Sanctions is contained in the French Government's presentation to the ICAO Legal Committee's special sub-committee.[45] While pointing out that France had adopted on 17 July 1970 a law specifically making aerial hijacking a crime punishable with penalties ranging from five years imprisonment to the death sentence; and that on 5 July 1972 a new law had extended French jurisdictional competence in these matters, the French Government offered substantial criticisms of the US Draft Convention as submitted in October 1970, and of the revised joint US-Canadian Draft Convention of April 1971. So far as both Drafts envisaged sanctions, including an air blockade, against delinquent States failing to comply with their obligations under Articles 7 and 8 of the Hague Convention, the French Government contended that under Article 41 of the United Nations Charter, the taking of collective sanctions against States, including in particular the ordering of an air blockade, was reserved exclusively to the UN Security Council (a legal position, incidentally, also advanced by the Soviet Union).

As a second legal objection, the French Government contended that the Hague Convention could establish legal obligations only for those States parties to it and therefore would permit imposing sanctions only on those parties,—this as a legal consequence of Articles 34 and 35 of the Vienna Convention on Treaties. The political conclusion from this would be that, in the absence of any ability legally to bind third

43. Non-enforcement Treaty. *New York Times*, 26 January 1973.
44. *New York Times*, 28 January 1973.
45. LC/Working Draft, No. 821, 15 December 1972.

parties who had not signed and ratified the Hague Convention, that Convention could only be really effective if and when it were universally accepted.

As a third legal point, the French objected that the establishment of machinery for sanctions would not be easily compatible with the conciliation and arbitration clauses found in various existing conventions, including the Hague Convention itself.

Finally, the French suggested that any decisions on the suspension of air services, such as would be implied by the imposition of an air blockade against a delinquent State, could not legally be taken without first amending the welter of bilateral agreements granting air traffic rights in relation to the delinquent State; and perhaps, also, without first amending the Chicago Convention of 1944.

It was on the basis of these objections that the French put forward their proposal,—which was to be included, in modified form, in the ICAO Legal Committee's recommendation, of January 1973, as to the subjects for two further conferences on sanctions—to make the provisions of the Hague Convention obligatory for all ICAO member-States, under penalty of expulsion from ICAO. This, it was contended, could be attained by using the procedure specified in Article 94 of the Chicago Convention as to amendment of that Convention,—a procedure to be initiated by a two-thirds majority vote of the ICAO Assembly and which specifically authorises the Assembly to provide, in its resolution recommending adoption of an amendment, that any State not ratifying the amendment within a specified period shall automatically cease to be a member of ICAO and to be a party to the Chicago Convention.[46] The thrust of the French argument here was that the

46. Chicago Convention of 1944. Convention on International Civil Aviation:

"Article 94. Amendment of Convention.

(a) Any proposed amendment to this Convention must be approved by a two-thirds vote of the Assembly and shall then come into force in respect of States which have ratified such amendment when ratified by the number of contracting States specified by the Assembly. The number so specified shall not be less than two-thirds of the total number of contracting States.

(b If in its opinion the amendment is of such a nature as to justify this course, the Assembly in its resolution recommending adoption may provide that any State which has not ratified within a specified period after the amendment has come into force shall thereupon cease to be a member of the Organisation and a party to the Convention."

And see generally J. Erler, *Rechtsfragen der ICAO* (1967), pp. 92-107.

Chicago Convention be amended with a view to incorporating in it Articles 1 to 11 of the Hague Convention.

In essence, the French case was that they agreed with the objective of the US-Canadian Draft, but that they didn't like the US-Canadian method of approach: their own method, by comparison, the French argued, would not disregard either the Chicago Convention or the plethora of bilateral air agreements concluded under its general *aegis*. The French also claimed their method to involve the most severe sanction of all—expulsion from ICAO—and that without the need for amending the United Nations Charter, as (according to the particular argument) would be necessary to give legal validity to the substance of the US-Canadian sanctions proposals.

By way of review of the political and legal merits of these French counter-proposals, it may be suggested that the contention that only the United Nations Security Council is legally competent, in terms of Article 41 of the UN Charter, to apply collective sanctions (including an air blockade), is at least open to question.[47] Again, in contending that the specific obligations contained in the Hague Convention are applicable only to States parties to that Convention, the French brief may take too conservative a view which ignores, among other things, the extent to which those obligations may exist as general (customary or other) international law principles anterior to and independent of the Hague Convention.[48] Finally, in suggesting, as a viable approach to enforcement of the Hague and related Conventions, the roundabout route of amendment of the Chicago Convention with a view to incorporating therein Articles 1 to 11 of the Hague Convention and also incorporating a provision for automatic expulsion from ICAO

---

47. The countervailing argument, surely, is that the UN Charter in terms gives the Security Council "primary", but certainly not exclusive, responsibility for the maintenance of international peace and security. See the response to the French and Soviet arguments, in the specific context of sanctions against States aiding or abetting hijackers, made by Stephen M. Schwebel, former Assistant Legal Adviser, US State Department. Letter to the Editor, *New York Times,* 16 September 1972.

48. Thus Judge Lachs, in his Dissenting Opinion in the *North Sea Continental Shelf* cases, concluded that West Germany should be regarded as being bound by the principles of the Geneva Convention on the Continental Shelf of 1958, even though West Germany had merely signed, *though not ratified,* the Convention. As Judge Lachs noted, in his Dissenting Opinion:

> "... The principles and rules enshrined in the Convention, and in particular the equidistance rule, have been accepted not only by those States which are parties to the Convention on the Continental Shelf, but also by

of States not ratifying that amendment, the French delegation is surely being rather arch. The amendment procedure for the Chicago Convention requires a two-thirds majority of the ICAO Assembly as its first step; and the difficulties experienced by the ICAO Assembly in other political *causes célèbres* of recent years in trying to build even a bare majority in support of rational and resolute proposals with teeth in them, suggest that this approach would be difficult and long-delayed in its attempted execution. In short, it seems substantially less concrete and immediate, and also very much weaker in its expected practical

---

those which have subsequently followed it in agreements, or in their legislation, or have acquiesced in it when faced with legislative acts of other States affecting them. This can be viewed as evidence of a practice widespread enough to satisfy the criteria for a general rule of law.

For to become binding, a rule or principle of international law need not pass the test of universal acceptance. This is reflected in several statements of the Court, e.g.: "generally ... adopted in the practice of States" (*Fisheries, Judgment, I.C.J. Reports 1951,* p. 128). Not all States have, as I indicated earlier in a different context, an opportunity or possibility of applying a given rule. The evidence should be sought in the behaviour of a great number of States, possibly the majority of States, in any case the great majority of the interested States....

As for uniformity, 'too much importance need not be attached to' a 'few uncertainties or contradictions, real and apparent' (*Fisheries, Judgment, I.C.J. Reports 1951,* p. 138).

Nor can a general rule which is not of the nature of *jus cogens* prevent some States from adopting an attitude apart. They may have opposed the rule from its inception and may, unilaterally, or in agreement with others, decide upon different solutions of the problem involved. Article 6, paragraph 2, of the Convention on the Continental Shelf, by virtue of the built-in exceptions, actually opens the way to occasional departures from the equidistance rule wherever special circumstances arise. Thus the fact that some States, as pointed out in the course of the proceedings, have enacted special legislation or concluded agreements at variance with the equidistance rule and the practice confirming it represents a mere permitted derogation and cannot be held to have disturbed the formation of a general rule of law on delimitation."

International Court of Justice, 1969, *Reports of Judgments, Judgment of 20 February 1969.* North Sea Continental Shelf cases (Federal Republic of Germany/Denmark; Federal Republic of Germany/Netherlands), p. 1; pp. 219 *et seq.* (Dissenting Opinion of Judge Lachs), at pp. 229-230.

As to treaties and Third States generally, see the *Free Zones of Upper Savoy and the District of Gex,* PCIJ, Ser. A/B, No. 46, p. 96 (1932); 2 Hudson, *World Court Reports* 508 (1935); *Vienna Convention on the Law of Treaties,* 1969, Articles 34, 35, 36, 37; R. F. Roxburgh, *International Conventions and Third States* (1917); Jiménez de Aréchaga, "Treaty Stipulations in Favour of Third States", *American Journal of International Law,* Vol. 50 (1956), p. 338; Hans Ballreich, "Verträge zugunsten und zu lasten Dritter", Strupp-Schlochauer (editors), *Wörterbuch des Völkerrechts,* Vol. 3, p. 544.

effects, than the US-Canadian Draft, without in any real way offering advantages in terms of speed-up of the political processes of its adoption.

2. The Treaty Route: the Bilateral Treaty (or Limited, Regional Accord) Approach

The failure of action of a multilateral character—specifically, the practical failure, up to date, to control aerial hijacking through multilateral conventions—brings into relief the comparative success achieved with deliberately more limited action, here action of a bilateral or limited, regional character. The United States-Cuban accord signed on 15 February 1973, is not formally styled as a treaty, but simply as a Memorandum of Understanding on hijacking of aircraft and vessels and other offences.[49] But in practical terms it seems to amount to very much the same thing.

It will be remembered that early in 1961 there had been suggestions of a US-Cuban accord on the hijacking problem, as the first US civil passenger aircraft began to be hijacked to Cuba. The difficulties, at that time, in reaching a formal accord seem to have been not so much ideological—and this in spite of the estrangement between the two countries following on the Cuban Government's expropriation of American-owned property in Cuba, and in spite also of the mutual withdrawal of diplomatic missions—as practical and humanitarian difficulties for the United States Government. In the flood of anti-Castro Cuban refugees reaching the United States mainland at that period were numbers who had seized aircraft or, more usually, small ships and boats, as a means of escape from Cuba. The Cuban Government insisted on full reciprocity to the extent that, in exchange for the extradition or forced return from Cuba to the United States of persons who might have hijacked American civil aircraft to Cuba, they insisted that the US Government return any anti-Castro refugees who might have hijacked Cuban planes or vessels in escaping to the United States.

---

49. Cuba-United States: Memorandum of Understanding on the Hijacking of Aircraft and Vessels. Exchange of notes at Washington and Havana, 15 February 1973. Published in the *New York Times,* 16 February 1973; *International Legal Materials,* Vol. 12 (March 1973), pp. 370 *et seq.* (The exchange of diplomatic notes in Washington took place between the US Secretary of State, and the Chargé d'Affaires of the Czechoslovakian Embassy which represents Cuban interests in the US. The exchange of diplomatic notes in Havana was between the Swiss Ambassador, representing the United States, and the Cuban Minister of Foreign Affairs, *ibid.*)

Such a *quid pro quo* was clearly unacceptable in the light of the political attitudes prevailing in the United States at the beginning of the 1960s and the strong public opposition in the United States to Fidel Castro, so that it was not persevered with at the time. Instead, the principal efforts in both countries were focussed on the far less controversial issues of ensuring the prompt release and return to their home country of innocent passengers and crew of the hijacked plane or vessel who did not wish to remain in the country to which they had been hijacked; and of securing the return of the hijacked plane or vessel itself. These efforts, conducted on a highly pragmatic basis of mutuality and reciprocal self-interest, achieved a high degree of success, yielding a *de facto,* non-formal understanding or accord that was operated between the United States and Cuba, quietly and without too many political strains, for more than a decade until replaced by the formal Memorandum of Understanding of February 1973. (The *de facto,* informal US-Cuban bilateral accord is discussed more fully below.)[50]

The US-Cuban formal accord, or Memorandum of Understanding of 15 February 1973 followed some months of secret negotiations which were first hinted at, in the press, at the beginning of November 1972. The agreement was officially handled through the intermediary of the Swiss Minister in Havana who now represents American interests in Cuba; but there seems little doubt that it was preceded by very extensive direct American-Cuban contacts.

The US-Cuban Memorandum of Understanding is stated, in its preamble, to proceed—"on the basis of equality and strict reciprocity".

According to the opening Article of the accord:

> "Any person who hereafter seizes, removes, appropriates or diverts from its normal route or activities an aircraft or vessel registered under the laws of one of the parties and brings it to the territory of the other party shall be considered to have committed an offence and therefore shall either be returned to the party of registration of the aircraft or vessel to be tried by the courts of that party in conformity with its laws or be brought before the courts of the party whose territory he reached for trial in conformity with its laws for the offence punishable by the most severe penalty . . ."

50. See Chapter 3, *3, infra.*

This is, of course, the *aut dedere, aut punire* principle, as reflected in the Hague Convention of 1970, and specifically Article 7 of the Convention, though it is perhaps more tightly drafted than the Hague Convention so as to allow little room for a State to avoid seeing that a criminal delinquent is effectively prosecuted.

In addition, under the opening article of the accord, the party whose territory is reached by the aircraft or vessel is to—

> "take all necessary steps to facilitate without delay the continuation of the journey of the passengers and crew innocent of the hijacking of the aircraft or vessel in question, with their belongings, as well as the journey of the aircraft or vessel itself with all goods carried with it, including any funds obtained by extortion or other illegal means . . ."

This, once again, is a reflection of the principles of earlier Conventions—specifically Article 11 (2) of the Tokyo Convention and Article 9 (2) of the Hague Convention. But it is, once again also, more comprehensive than the earlier Conventions in specifying for the return of any funds extorted by the hijacker; and it is also far more precise in going on, also, to require the receiving State to—"take all steps to protect the physical integrity" of the hijacked aircraft or vessel and, more importantly, of the innocent passengers and crew. In these respects, certainly, the US-Cuban Memorandum of Understanding is, by any standards, a humane and modern accord; for it gives a very large degree of recognition to what is treated only rather imperfectly and indirectly in the Tokyo and the Hague Conventions and what was certainly flouted by numbers of States in the hijacking cases of recent years—namely, the principle of respect for the physical well-being and human dignity of the innocent passengers and crew of the hijacked craft as adumbrated in the *Institut de droit international's* resolution, at its Zagreb reunion in September 1971, which itself did no more, on this point, than re-state an already existing obligation of States under classical, customary international law.

The second article of the US-Cuban formal accord establishes an obligation on the part of each country to punish any person who, within its territory, conspires to promote or promotes an expedition which, from its territory or any other place, carries out acts of violence or depredation against aircraft or vessels coming or going to the territory of the other party; or who, within its territory, conspires to promote or promotes an expedition which carries out such acts or other similar unlawful acts in the territory of the other party. This particular provision is understood to have been directed principally towards alleged hit-and-run raids supposed from time to time to have been directed against Cuba by anti-Castro nationals or ex-nationals now living in the United States.

The fourth article of the formal accord is very important because it directs attention to the vexed issue of "political motives", the failure to resolve which was understood to have been a factor in delaying, for a decade, the achievement of the US-Cuban formal accord. The problem of the so-called "political exception" to compulsory extradition in hijacking cases is approached, in the fourth article, in a very contemporary way and without the very large loop-holes to effective punishment of hijackers to be found in some of the contemporary juristic discussion of the same question:

> "The party in whose territory the perpetrators of the acts ... first arrive may take into consideration any extenuating or mitigating circumstances in those cases in which the persons responsible for the acts were being sought for strictly political reasons and were in real and imminent danger of death without a viable alternative for leaving the country, provided there was no financial extortion or physical injury to the members of the crew, passengers, or other persons in connection with the hijacking."

There you have a very humane and modern formulation of the so-called "political exception". It is to exist, but only on the basis of going to extenuation or mitigation, and never presumably to the basic issue of criminality. Also, so far as it might go to extenuation or mitigation, it can only apply where there was real and imminent danger of death, without a viable alternative way of escape for the hijacker; and the hijacker, in any case, can only invoke it where he has committed no financial extortion or physical injury to the innocent passengers and aircrew and other persons. This latter condition picks up the highly nuanced reasoning of the Swiss Federal Supreme Court's decision of 1952 [51] where the important juridical principle is enunciated that the choice of means to effectuate a hijacking can indeed control the legitimacy of the ends sought to be attained, to the point

---

51. Decision of the Federal Supreme Court of Switzerland, 30 April 1952. 78 *Entscheidungen des Bundesgerichts* I, 39 (1952); *International Legal Reports*, Vol. 19 (1952), p. 371.

where impermissible means involving, for example, unnecessary or disproportionate use of force could operate to vitiate a claimed political objective altogether. And so in its own way, the US-Cuban formal accord is a healthy reminder, in a too often violent and lawless era of international relations, that an act otherwise justifiable on claimed "political" or other grounds may lose its legal justification if you use improper means; which, in the context of aerial hijacking, include of course gratuitously endangering or harming innocent passengers.

It remains to note that while, to date, the US-Cuban formal accord of 15 February 1973, on control of aerial hijacking, has not turned out to be the harbinger of a more general US-Cuban political *détente,* as some have suggested, it has been followed by hints that the US-Cuban text could serve as a model for similar bilateral accords between the United States and other countries known to be troubled, as Cuba certainly was, by a growing international reputation as a "haven" for emotional misfits and similar pathological cases or for international political trouble-makers. The *New York Times* carried a report that Algeria was interested in concluding a bilateral US-Algerian agreement on control of hijacking on a basis identical to the US-Cuban accord.[52] The report was interesting because it followed clear evidence of displeasure on the part of the Algerian Government over American expatriates living in Algeria who had either been involved in direct hijacking or who had collaborated with hijackers after the event. In August 1972 the Algerian Government insisted upon returning to the United States one and a half million dollars ransom that Eldridge Cleaver, leader of an "underground" militant movement in the United States, the Black Panthers, who was now in asylum in Algeria, had obtained as the proceeds of two hijackings of American civil passenger aircraft in the United States. The Algerian insistence on returning the ransom money to the United States seemed to presage tougher official action against hijackers seeking refuge in Algeria, the suggestion being that Algeria had weighed the merits and demerits of remaining a "haven" for "political" hijackers, and had decided that, on balance, there were too many risks involved in being a "haven", and that it just wasn't worth it.[53]

52. *New York Times,* 17 February 1973.

53. *International Herald Tribune* (Paris), 2 August 1972; the *Sunday Times* (London), 20 August 1972.

3. *The Bilateral Approach (continued): the Informal Accord or Consensus*

Sometimes, in international relations, the formal treaty route (whether multilateral or bilateral) to solution of a problem may not be practicable or even possible due to the lack of formal recognition of each other on the part of the principal States concerned, or the absence of formal diplomatic relations, or else a general condition of tension and political strain in diplomatic dealings between those States. The informal accord or consensus,—provided there are objective conditions ensuring that it will be honestly observed by each party, and this normally means only that it be based upon mutual and reciprocal self-interest—offers a way out of the impasse on a highly pragmatic and operational basis.

The US-Cuban Memorandum of Understanding of 15 February 1973 had been preceded, as we have noted, by more than a decade of practical accommodation between the two countries in regard to the release and return to their home country of civil aircraft and their passengers and aircrew hijacked from the one country to the other.[54]

Now the first hijacking of an American commercial aircraft to Cuba seems to have occurred on 1 May 1961, immediately after the United States' severance of diplomatic relations with the Castro Government in January 1961, following on the Castro decrees expropriating American-owned property in Cuba. The first hijacking involved a National Airlines Convair aircraft which was taken over while flying over Florida, by an armed Cuban who forced the pilot to fly the plane to Havana. The other passengers and the three crew members were allowed by the Cuban authorities to return to the United States in the same plane.

The second hijacking of an American commercial aircraft to Cuba took place on 24 July 1961, with far more serious political implications. It involved an Eastern Airlines Electra aircraft, taken over by a gunman on a flight from Miami, Florida, to Tampa, New Orleans, and Dallas, with 32 other passengers and 5 crew members on board. On arrival in Havana, the passengers and crew members were lodged

54. *Annuaire de l'Institut de droit international,* Vol. 54, I ("Hijacking of Aircraft") [1971], pp. 520 *et seq.*; A. F. Lowenfeld, *Aviation Law. Cases and Materials* (1972), Ch. 7. 1; A. Chayes, T. Ehrlich, and A. F. Lowenfeld, *International Legal Process. Materials for an Introductory Course* (1968), Vol. 1, pp. 88 *et seq.*

overnight in the airport hotel in Havana, and allowed to return to Miami the next day on a Pan American flight. The Electra aircraft itself, however, was detained by the Castro Government in Havana, apparently as some sort of *quid pro quo* for the fact that some 25 Cuban aircraft (18 of them hijacked by Cuban refugees from the Castro *régime*) had, since mid-1959, been seized by various judicial authorities in the United States in pursuance to American court orders. President Kennedy indicated, in a Press conference on 10 August 1961,[55] that 14 of these Cuban planes had, since their original judicial seizure, been returned to Cuba, and 9 of them sold in response to the court orders in satisfaction of property judgments rendered by US state courts. But President Kennedy also said that steps were being taken to ensure that the Cuban Government would raise the jurisdictional defence of sovereign immunity, in the future, in any proceedings involving its aircraft before American courts. On 12 August 1961, a US State Department press release indicated that the Electra plane would be released by the Castro Government on 15 August in response to the US Government's assertion of the claim of sovereign immunity in respect to a Cuban naval vessel which had recently been seized and brought into United States territorial waters by anti-Castro Cuban refugees.[56] On 16 August 1961, the deal was in fact completed, with the Electra plane returning to the United States and the Cuban patrol boat returning to Cuba.

While there may have been hopes that this *ad hoc* accord between the United States and Cuba would lead to an ending of the hijacking of American commercial aircraft to Cuba, this was not to be the case. The hijackers of American planes in these later cases turned out, all too frequently, to be mentally deranged or psychotic individuals acting on their own initiative and not in pursuance of any direct, governmental orders, most of them, indeed, seeming to be United States citizens. An elaborate, inter-governmental ritual appears, thereupon, to have been worked out between the United States and the Cuban authorities, acting through the good offices of the Swiss Consulate-General in Havana (which represents US interests in Cuba since the breaking off of US-Cuban diplomatic relations), to operate once a

55. *Chayes, Ehrlich, and Lowenfeld, op. cit.*, pp. 102-103.

56. See, in this regard, *Rich* v. *Naviera Vacuba, S.A.*, 197 F. Supp. 710 (E.D.Va. (1961)) (Hoffman, District Judge); 295 F. 2d 24 (4th Cir. (1961)) (Sobeloff CJ, Soper, and Bryan, Circuit Judges). More generally, see *Banco Nacional de Cuba* v. *Sabbatino,* 376 U.S., 398 [1964].

hijacked US commercial aircraft should have landed in Havana. Under these arrangements, the passengers and crew of the hijacked aircraft had to stay overnight in Havana but were then permitted to return to the United States the next day, on a different aircraft (a non-jet) from the one that they had arrived on and one specially flown in from the United States, with its crew, for the purpose. The unofficial explanation advanced by the Castro Government for this requirement was that most of the hijacked American commercial aircraft were jets and that the José Martí international airport at Havana was not properly equipped to handle the take-off of a jet aircraft fully loaded with its normal complement of air crew and passengers. The hijacked aircraft itself was, however, permitted to return to the United States, empty save for its crew. The Castro Government then proceeded to bill the American commercial airline company concerned, at commercial rates, for the hotel accommodations and the living expenses of the aircrew and passengers of the hijacked aircraft, and for the aircraft landing and take-off charges, the bill being transmitted to the US Government through the Swiss Consulate-General. The hijacker himself appeared, almost without exception, to be permitted by the Castro Government to remain in Cuba.

These elaborate arrangements were operated so many times over the more than a decade from 1961 to the conclusion of the formal US-Cuban Memorandum of Understanding of 15 February 1973, as to become almost a routine; for, over the years since 1961, the procedures seemed to have worked smoothly and effectively and with a minimum of public complaint on either side. The aircrews of American commercial passenger aircraft apparently had instructions not to resist armed hijackers, out of consideration for the safety of their passengers' lives; and the aircrews apparently were also issued with air route maps to Cuba and plans of the José Martí airport at Havana and even Spanish-language cards, to facilitate communications with hijackers.

Hijacking of planes in the Western Hemisphere has not been limited, of course, to United States commercial passenger aircraft. The most frequent victim, apart from the United States, has been Colombia; and there have also been hijackings involving the aircraft of Brazil, Ecuador, Mexico, Peru and Venezuela. A hijacking of an American (Pan American World Airways) jet aircraft, on 9 August 1961 in Mexican air space, however, produced a quick show-down between the Mexican Government and Cuba, facilitated by Cuba's effective political and commercial dependence on Mexico as the only country in the

Americas still maintaining a regular, scheduled commercial passenger service to Cuba: after a French national, Cadon—identified by US President Kennedy, in his press conference on 10 August 1961, as having undergone medical treatment in New York earlier in the same year for mental aberrations—had hijacked the aircraft over Mexico on a flight from Mexico City to Guatemala, with the Colombian Foreign Minister among the passengers, the Castro Government, at the demand of the Mexican Government, not merely released the aircraft and its passengers and aircrew, but also surrendered the hijacker himself for extradition to Mexico to face trial on charges of robbery and illegal possession of firearms. This seems to have been the only instance in which the Cuban Government—up to the formal US-Cuban Memorandum of Understanding of 15 February 1973, at least—has surrendered the hijacker himself to the country of nationality of the aircraft that has been hijacked; and, in the particular case, it was reported that the hijacker, Cadon, was sentenced by the Mexican courts to 8 years and 9 months' imprisonment.

The Cuban hijackings, no doubt because of the joint, bilaterally-initiated, perfectioning of the arrangements for the speedy release of passengers and aircrew and the hijacked aircraft itself, took on, over the years from 1961 on, something of the public appearance of an interesting and harmless adventure—even of a sort of humorous relief from the routine ease and comfort of contemporary jet-age commercial passenger air travel. On the other hand, it must not be overlooked that there was also not inconsiderable passenger inconvenience, very great additional commercial operating costs, and the occasional serious injury or fatality resulting from the hijacking attempts, not to mention the ever-present hazard of an aerial catastrophe resulting from the excitement of the events surrounding the hijacking act itself and from the usually high-strung emotional condition of the hijacker. Perhaps it was the comic opera character of the Cuban *genre* of hijacking, stemming in part from the very inequality in political, military, and economic power of Cuba and of the United States respectively, that accounted for the substantial failure of the World Community, at least in the early and middle 1960s when the incidence of hijackings, as a world phenomenon, was primarily limited to the "Cuban" cases, to take any really effective measures to prevent those hijackings from continuing.

With the gradual substantial improvement of the technical facilities (including, especially, facilities for take-off of aircraft), at the José

Martí international airport in Havana, even the smooth arrangements already developed through joint, US-Cuban, bilateral initiative, were able to be still further streamlined, to the point where the passengers and aircrew of a hijacked aircraft could now return to the United States in the originally hijacked plane, without any necessity to change planes or to remain in Havana overnight. The Cuban Government apparently now limited itself, because of this, to aircraft landing and take-off charges against the United States. Cases of "hijacking for gain" involving the extortion of ransom money by the hijackers, are apparently rare to the point almost of non-existence in the case of hijackings to Cuba; though the Cuban Government, in at least one recent case, seems to have seized the ransom money itself on the claim of applying it in satisfaction of outstanding Cuban claims against the United States.

On the whole, the United States-Cuban informal accord as to control of hijacking—preceding the formal accord of 15 February 1973—appears, in historical retrospect, to have worked to the satisfaction of both sides. It managed to avoid any unpleasant further escalation of originally very strained US-Cuban relations stemming from the other, broader issues of ideological and general political conflict between the two countries as Castro's commitment to the Soviet camp had become clear. And as far as the actual details of implementation of the US-Cuban informal accord on hijacking were concerned, each side seemed to believe that, on balance, the inconveniences involved—in the US case, payment to Cuba of the landing and take-off and related charges for hijacked aircraft, and tolerance of Cuba as a "haven" for the delinquent hijackers—were well worth the gain, in return, of safe and speedy return of the hijacked aircraft and its aircrew and passengers. It is worth noting, in regard to Cuba, that there have never been any of the complaints encountered in regard to hijackings to some other countries, of wilful or perverse mistreatment of the innocent aircrew and passengers on the part of the host or receiving country to which the hijacked aircraft was directed.

4. International Private Action:
International Commercial or Professional Associations

(a) *The International Air Transport Association (IATA)*

IATA's role as an international private, non-governmental, commercial association has already been referred to in some detail. IATA's secretariat can,—in terms of taking concrete, operational measures to control or counter hijacking,—presumably be no stronger than the collective will of its component parts, the individual national airline companies or organisations making up its membership. Nevertheless, in terms of public education through public discussions and public debate, IATA has always been active and vocal. In a press statement of 13 January 1969 the IATA Director-General, Knut Hammarskjöld, called for government support to have hijacking and similar acts of armed intervention delcared as "international crimes comparable to piracy and genocide", and he also called on UN member-nations to bring criminal charges against those committing such offences.[57]

In a further statement issued on 2 September 1969, the Director-General, while recognising the existence of a small number of hard-core political hijackings, claimed that the vast majority of cases were the work of mentally unbalanced or abnormal persons, and that an effective absence of both international and national legislation to deal with the problem left a gap in the law for mentally unbalanced or unstable people. He also sounded a warning as to the general utility of the treaty-based approach to solution of the hijacking problem:

> "... the inevitably slow process of signing and ratifying an international convention, which as experience shows can take many years, does not lead us to believe that a quick solution lies in this field".[58]

The Director-General of IATA did, however, in a further statement of 17 September 1969, propose that any United Nations measures against hijacking of civil air transport should include condemnation of such acts by declaring them to be international crimes equivalent to piracy on the high seas or genocide.[59]

The fatal bomb explosion of 23 February 1970, which destroyed a Swissair aircraft in flight, and the similar bomb explosion on board an Austrian Airlines aircraft, spurred IATA to measures of a more immediate and low-level character, and (more importantly) with far more concrete application than general resolutions. The Director-General of IATA called for increased police and security protection at

57. *Annuaire de l'Institut de droit international,* Vol. 54, I ("Hijacking of Aircraft") (1971), pp. 520 *et seq.*
58. *Ibid.*
59. *Ibid.*

airports, particularly at transit airports which he described as the "weak links in the chain of counter-actions". (Statement of 23 February 1970.) This was followed by a special meeting of IATA's Executive Committee which called for reinforced measures directed against the "proliferation of aggression against civil aircraft". (Statement of 9 March 1970.) The IATA Executive Committee proposals called, here, for action at three different levels of authority; by the political arm of government; by the civil airport administrations; and finally, by IATA's own members, the commercial airline companies. On the part of the political arm of government, IATA asked for international legislation to make unlawful seizure of an aircraft an international offence with severe penalties to be imposed, even prior to considering any request for political asylum; and for international legislation punishing the placing of explosives on board an aircraft. On the part of the civil airport administrations, IATA called for proper co-ordination of airport security amongst all interested governmental agencies (postal authorities, customs and immigration departments, local police and law enforcement officials); for security measures such as the searching or screening of passengers, and the examination of air baggage and cargo by means of decompression chambers, X-ray equipment, chemical detectors; and for screening of all forms of airmail letters and packages. On the part of airlines, IATA asked for maximum possible exchange of information on security, for standardisation of security measures, and for an effective liaison between airlines, civil airport administrations, and all governmental agencies concerned with the security and safety of air transport and air communications generally.[60]

This part, at least, of IATA's response to the aerial hijacking problem seems to have been very effective. For from these detailed IATA proposals stemmed both specific measures like the hijackers' "profile" developed as an aid to identification and detection of hijackers while they were still going through the on-the-ground ticketing and preboarding procedures, and so directed to "prevention before the act"; and also more general and comprehensive measures such as the airline companies' own pre-flight screening and search procedures for passengers and baggage, which were developed by the individual airlines even before such controls began to be made obligatory and uniform by governmental statute or administrative order, the effectiveness and

60. *Annuaire de l'Institut de droit international, op. cit.*, pp. 520 *et seq.*

range of such individual airline's measures depending of course upon the initiative and the sense of public responsibility and, not least, the economic resources of the airlines concerned.

(b) *The International Federation of Airline Pilots Associations (IFALPA)*

We have already discussed the highly successful intervention by IFALPA in the case of the July 1968 hijacking of an El Al aircraft to Algiers, when IFALPA's threat of a boycott on the part of its members of all flights into and out of Algeria had been followed, almost immediately, by the release of the El Al aircraft and its crew and the remaining passengers who had been detained by the Algerian authorities for a six-weeks' period following the original hijacking of the aircraft to Algiers.

IFALPA, at its Amsterdam conference in March 1969, had adopted a special resolution under the title "Freedom of Transit—Hijacking of Civil Aircraft",[61] which castigated the various national governments for their sustained inactivity in regard to the control of hijacking and predicted a "major catastrophe" unless that governmental inaction were reversed. More important, however, the resolution went on to authorise the principal officers of IFALPA to initiate appropriate action against States "failing to institute appropriate punishment" against a hijacker illegally diverting an aircraft to their territory. Such action could include action to:

> "Ban all traffic into the offending State;
>
> Effect co-ordination with other organisations to restrict the movement of aircraft of the offending State and further to restrict the movement of cargo to and from the offending State, whether it be by air or surface transport."

IFALPA members soon had occasion to test their own seriousness in regard to their resolution, with the hijacking of a TWA airliner to Syria on 29 August 1969, and the subsequent detention by the Syrian Government of two Israeli civilians who had been on the hijacked aircraft. IFALPA threatened to call a pilots' strike against Syria; and in a long and complicated diplomatic manœuvre in which IFALPA withdrew its strike threat at the personal request of UN Secretary-

---

61. *Annuaire de l'Institut de droit international,* Vol. 54, I ("Hijacking of Aircraft") (1971), pp. 520 *et seq.*

General U Thant, Syria finally released the two Israeli civilians on 5 December 1969.[62]

IFALPA was later also to protest at the Israeli Government's arrest of two Algerian passengers at the Tel Aviv airport, following on an unscheduled stop there by a BOAC aircraft *en route* from Karachi to London, the two Algerian passengers being subsequently released by the Israeli Government. IFALPA also demanded the extradition to Czechoslovakia, to face trial, of two Czechoslovak nationals who hijacked a small Czechoslovak airliner to West Germany on 7 June 1972, and who had killed the pilot and wounded two passengers in the process.[63]

IFALPA, in its Amsterdam resolution of March 1969, had also approved the principle of a world-wide 12 to 24 hours' general strike by airline pilots, "to focus public attention on this most pressing problem of air safety"; and the one-day world-wide pilots' strike of 19 June 1972,[64] which finally triggered a belated inter-governmental initiative in terms of an ICAO Legal Committee meeting to study the issue of sanctions against delinquent States harbouring or otherwise aiding hijackers, was an eventual consequence of this resolution.

By and large, however, IFALPA's potential to curb or control the hijacking problem seems hardly to have been used to the full. With a membership of 44,000 pilots in 54 countries, IFALPA's ability to mount a crippling, if not necessarily complete, boycott against a delinquent State is clearly there, as was demonstrated in the Algerian case in 1968. Beyond that, as a professional skill group with highly developed expertise in the area of air security and air safety, IFALPA's collective views and recommendations must command the respect of governments concerned with the same questions: hence the intellectual weight of the further IFALPA recommendations, at the March 1969 Amsterdam conference, that its members pressure their own national governments not to conclude or to renew bilateral air transport agreements with other States unless such bilateral agreements include a firm reciprocal undertaking either to apprehend, prosecute, and punish hijackers landing in their territory or to return the hijackers to the State of registration of the aircraft for prosecution.

---

62. I. M. Sheppard, "Air Piracy: the Rôle of the International Federation of Airline Pilots Associations", *Cornell International Law Journal,* Vol. 3 (1970), p. 79, at pp. 79-80.

63. *New York Times (Sunday),* 11 June 1972.

64. *Le Devoir* (Montreal), 17 June 1972; *New York Times,* 17 June 1972.

The threat of a boycott by IFALPA's members against a delinquent State remains as a reserve control, to be used, if need be, in default of affirmative and effective control action by the organised political community, both international and national, against hijackers. As an informal control, and one moreover that implies self-help style, direct action, it is subject to all the doubts that jurists traditionally attach to self-help as a crude and unsophisticated, and ultimately dangerous, form of social control. But its potential effects are immense and relatively immediate. And if to the airline pilots' options for direct action there be added the extra weight of much larger and financially far more powerful organisations such as the International Transport Workers Federation—an association of airport trade unions representing 250,000 workers in 21 countries, that has threatened to stop servicing airlines "destined for any country that aids or gives sanctuary to hijackers or saboteurs",[65] then the chances of applying effective, if informal community sanctions against delinquent States seem very real and also immediate.

5. *National Action*

(a) *National Action in Regard to Bilateral Air Transport Agreements*

Each State retains the right, in making new bilateral air transport agreements or in renewing existing ones, to insist on inserting in the agreements a special clause conditioning the existence of the agreement as a whole or else the continued enjoyment of the landing rights facilities created under it, upon adherence to and *bona fide* compliance with the various hijacking control treaties such as the Tokyo, the Hague, and the Montreal Conventions; or upon acceptance by the other contracting State of the principle, *aut dedere aut punire*. It may be argued, beyond this, that a State might move unilaterally to revoke already existing bilateral transport agreements on *clausula rebus sic stantibus*-style arguments that the other contracting State, in harbouring or otherwise aiding hijackers, had violated principles of the "freedom of the air" on which the bilateral agreement concerned, and indeed the plethora of inter-connected and inter-related bilateral agreements taken as a whole, are predicated. It is perhaps a commen-

65. *The Economist* (London), 2-8 January 1971.

tary upon the sense of collective solidarity existing among States in regard to the vindication of the principle of the "freedom of the air", and upon the apparently ingrained tendency to wait upon collective action—even if to wait may be to wait in vain, that up to date, no State (and among these the major commercial air traffic States such as the United States, Great Britain, France, the Netherlands, that have the commercially choicest and most sought-after air landing rights to concede) has yet ventured upon a unilateral initiative to condition its making or renewal of its bilateral air transport agreements with other States upon, in effect, a "good neighbour" standard of conduct on the part of those other States in respect to the pursuit and punishment of aerial hijacking. An ambitious attempt in the United States—which had impressive support in both the Senate and the House of Representatives at the time of its initiation in the Summer of 1972—would have closed US airports to any international airline serving countries offering a haven to hijackers: the plan of the legislative measure was a scheme of primary and secondary boycotts against countries harbouring hijackers or countries continuing to conduct airline services with countries harbouring hijackers, by both cancelling US airline flights to those countries and also denying their airlines landing facilities in the United States.[66] Although the proposed measure seemed to have overwhelming public backing in the United States, apart from the impressive Congressional support offered in advance, the measure ran into unexpected political difficulties and by the Autumn of 1972 had become a non-event.[67] It was widely suggested that the key was the US President's conclusion that the United States could not afford, in effect, to "go it alone", in applying sanctions measures against delinquent countries or their associates.[68]

---

66. A tough anti-hijacking bill provided for a new airport security police force, screening of all airline passengers, and the option of imposing the death penalty for hijackers, and also gave the US President the authority to suspend service of a US airline to a foreign country, or service of a foreign airline to the United States, if the foreign country concerned aided or harboured hijackers or hosted or aided terrorist groups who used air piracy as a weapon; or if the foreign country did not take adequate precautions to guard against hijacking; or if the foreign country continued its service to another country that aided or abetted hijackers or sky terrorists. The bill was adopted by the US Senate by a vote of 75 to 1, and sent on to the lower House. *New York Times,* 22 September 1972.

67. *New York Times,* 14 October 1972.

68. *New York Times,* 23 September 1972; *ibid.,* 26 September 1972; *ibid.,* 30 September 1972.

(b) *National Penal Laws*

In view of the relative newness of the act of aerial hijacking, very few countries have as yet passed laws specifically and in terms dealing with the offence of hijacking, as such. Where the hijacking is accompanied by actual violence visited upon the aircrew or passengers, or by robbery from their persons or luggage, any country having jurisdiction under its own national laws could—on condition, of course, of being able first of all to apprehend or otherwise to obtain physical control over the hijacker—no doubt easily apply existing standard provisions of its Criminal Code or other criminal laws covering those offences. It might also be possible to apply existing national laws covering such offences as unlawful detention, kidnapping, and abduction. Prior to the passage, in 1961, of a special amendment to the Federal Aviation Act of 1958, for example, the United States Justice Department tried to reach cases of aerial hijacking by prosecuting the hijackers on such charges as transporting a stolen aircraft in interstate commerce, kidnapping the persons aboard, or obstructing commerce by threats of violence.[69]

In 1961 the US Congress amended the Federal Aviation Act to provide for the offence of "aircraft piracy", defined as being—

> "any seizure or exercise of control, by force or violence or threat of force or violence and with wrongful intent, of an aircraft in flight in air commerce".

The offence of aircraft piracy, as so defined, is to be punishable by the death penalty (presumably, now become an invalid provision, in the light of a recent US Supreme Court ruling on the unconstitutionality of the death penalty);[70] or, failing that, by imprisonment for not less than 20 years.

Assaulting, intimidating, or threatening any flight crew member or flight attendant (including any steward or stewardess) while aboard an aircraft, is subject to a fine of up to $ 10,000 or imprisonment of up to 20 years, or both; with even heavier penalties, up to life imprisonment, for using a deadly or dangerous weapon in the commission of any such act.

---

69. See, in this regard, *Bearden* v. *U.S.*, 330 F. 2d. 99 [1963]; *cert.* denied, 376 U.S. 922 [1964].

70. See *Furman* v. *Georgia*, 92 S. Ct. 2726 [1972].

Having on one's person while aboard an aircraft any concealed deadly or dangerous weapon; or attempting to board an aircraft with any such concealed deadly or dangerous weapon, is (except in the case of specified law enforcement officers) subject to a fine of up to $ 1,000 or imprisonment of up to one year, or both.

While the existence of the new offence of "aircraft piracy" has hardly, of itself, been enough to control the aerial hijacking problem, the 1961 Air Piracy amendment to the Federal Aviation Act does have a considerable record of punitive application, after the event; though against a background of widely varying penalties as applied by individual judges. In the decade from 1961 to 1971, it is recorded that out of 117 incidents of actual or attempted hijackings (94 successful and 23 unsuccessful hijackings) 32 persons were brought to trial in the United States, including 15 persons who had returned from Cuba, with 92 individuals still listed as fugitives in connection with those hijacking incidents.[71] Of those tried in the United States, 1 was convicted of aircraft piracy and also of kidnapping and sentenced to life imprisonment on each count;[72] 1 was sentenced to 50 years' imprisonment for air piracy; 5 were sentenced to 20 years for air piracy or interference with commerce; and 9 others to terms of imprisonment ranging from 25 years to as low as 2 years. The cases of 11 other defendants were disposed of for reasons of insanity, on various grounds —dismissal, acquittal, commitment to state mental institutions; and five persons were sentenced under the Youth Corrections Act.[73] It is, of course, a very wide range of sentences and indicates not merely the multiplicity of different, co-ordinate federal criminal jurisdictions, but also the widely varying attitudes towards crime and punishment held on the part of individual federal judges.

In addition to the United States, such widely differing countries as Cuba and France have enacted special hijacking control legislation.

The Cuban Law, promulgated on 16 September 1969,[74]—possibly in anticipation of renewed diplomatic negotiations as to a US-Cuban hijacking control agreement, opens up with a very lengthy Preamble which is remarkable for its denunciation of hijacking. Among the recitals in the Preamble:

---

71. Lowenfeld, *op. cit.,* Ch. 7, 21.
72. *U.S.* v. *Ervin,* 436 F.2d. 1331 [1971].
73. Lowenfeld, *op. cit.,* Ch. 7, 21-2.
74. Discussed in *Annuaire de l'Institut de droit international,* Vol. 54, I ("Hijacking of Aircraft") (1971), pp. 520 *et seq.*

"... Diversions by force of ships and planes from their normal routes and activities jeopardise the lives of innocent people, adversely affect air and sea navigation activities, infringe national and international laws ...

Although in a few cases the hijackings have been caused by persons in real danger because of their political activities, in other instances they have been the work of common criminals, persons of immoral conduct, the mentally unbalanced or socially maladjusted, eager to change their country of residence, or those motivated by strictly personal reasons that cannot be classified in any way as revolutionary ..."

The Cuban Law is stipulated as applying, *inter alia,* to the—

"diverting a ship or plane from its normal route or activities by deceit, bribery, violence, or intimidation, or in connivance with any member of the crew". (Article 1 *(b)*);

and to the—

"jeopardising the safety of a ship or plane, of the persons or property on board, of third parties, or the order and discipline within such plane or ship". (Article 1 *(c)*.)

The Cuban law goes on to declare that persons committing any of these acts who arrive in Cuba may be returned to the State affected by their acts if they are claimed by that State (Article 2); but that these measures shall apply solely on bases of equality and strict reciprocity with respect to the States affected that enter into a bilateral agreement with Cuba on the application of the same policy (Article 3). When Cuban nationals are involved, Cuba reserves the right to apply its own legal measures (Article 4). Finally, Cuba reserves the right to grant asylum, when it deems it to be justified, to persons coming to Cuba for political reasons—

"having found it necessary to employ extreme means in order to escape from a real danger of death or grave repression" (Article 5).

The French Law, which was adopted as an amendment to the *Code Pénal,* on 15 July 1970, punishes the taking control of an aircraft in flight, by violence or the threat of violence, with imprisonment for a term of 5 to 10 years; and if such action results in injury or in death, the punishment is to be from 10 to 20 years' imprisonment or life imprisonment, respectively (Article 462, as amended).[75]

The new Soviet law on hijacking—Decree of the USSR Supreme Soviet on criminal liability for the Hijacking of Aircraft—adopted on 3 January 1973, provides that hijacking of aircraft, on the ground or in flight, is to be punished by imprisonment for a period of 3 to 10 years. The same act, or the seizure of an aircraft for the purpose of hijacking, when committed with the use of violence or threats or when resulting in the crash of the aircraft or other grave consequences, are to be punished by imprisonment for 5 to 15 years, with or without confiscation of property. The same actions, when they result in loss of life or serious bodily injury, are to be punished by imprisonment for 8 to 15 years, with confiscation of property; or by the death penalty, with confiscation of property. *Concealment* of these crimes, and *failure to report* knowledge of the crimes in preparation or already committed, are also to be punished by terms of imprisonment.[76] It is noted that according to Soviet law—as indeed with other systems of law—not only is the committing of these crimes punishable, but also preparing to commit or attempting to commit the crimes.[77]

(c) *National Administrative and Police Control Measures*

(i) On-the-ground, pre-flight screenings and searches of passengers and luggage

Our focus shifts now to attempts to control the hijacking problem by prevention measures on-the-ground and in advance of the flight, this as a direct consequence both of the failure, up to date, to achieve viable international controls, and also of the fact that national penal processes, even when coupled with effective extradition procedures, operate inevitably *ex post facto* when the damage has already been done.

While a number of international commercial airline companies have voluntarily introduced preventive, pre-flight, on-the-ground, anti-hijacking measures—some of these—for example, the measures im-

---

75. Loi no. 70-634 du 15 juillet 1970, insérant dans le code pénal un article 462 réprimant le détournement d'aéronef (J.O. 17 juill., p. 6657) (1); *Recueil Dalloz Sirey*, 31 août 1970.

76. Published in *Pravda*, 4 January 1973; *Izvestiya*, 4 January 1973.

77. See V. Ivanov, "Against Air Pirates", *Izvestiya*, 16 January 1973.

posed by El Al—being extraordinarily effective if we judge them by their concrete results in eliminating potential hijackings—we shall concentrate on the preventive measures developed and applied in the United States for the reason that these measures are now expressly sanctioned by federal governmental authority; and also because, having regard to the sheer volume of air traffic in the United States, the legal and other problems attendant upon such preventive measures have been clearly and frequently demonstrated, in litigation and otherwise.

The preventive, pre-flight, on-the-ground, control measures in the United States were actually begun by a number of commercial airlines on their own initiative, and with varying degrees of enthusiasm and thoroughness, depending in part on the financial resources of the airline companies concerned. For the most part, they were limited to some form of scrutiny (electronic or manual) of the passenger's carry-on, hand luggage, with or without some form of electronic, metal-detector test applied to the passenger's person. On 5 December 1972, however, the United States Government issued an emergency order requiring all US commercial airlines, by 5 January 1973, to institute a search of all passengers' carry-on luggage, and also to search all passengers electronically for possession of weapons.[78] The US administration further required that, by 5 February 1973, each of the nation's 531 commercial airports should station an armed officer from a local law enforcement agency, at boarding gates before every airline flight.[79] In announcing the plan, the US administration indicated that it expected that the travelling public should pay for the tighter airport security—this probably through the imposition of higher air fares. In announcing the measures, the US Assistant-Secretary of Transportation, Benjamin O. Davis, indicated that the US airlines, in addition to screening their passengers electronically and searching all carry-on luggage, must also ensure that armed guards would be available for every departure of planes from foreign airports; for where simple screening of passengers might have deterred hijackers in the past, with a new breed of hijackers "unequal in their ruthlessness and their wanton disregard for human life", one must be ready to stop them forcefully at the boarding gate.[80]

While the new compulsory search and screening measures were immediately welcomed by the Airline Pilots Association, they were,

78. *New York Times,* 6 December 1972.
79. *Ibid.*
80. *Ibid.*

initially, given only luke-warm support by the airline industry, and were strongly criticised by the Association of Airport Operators, mainly on account of the cost factor and the still undetermined question of who would have to bear the extra financial burden—the federal government, state and city governments, or (as was feared) the commercial airlines of the individual airport administrations themselves. This additional cost was projected, at the time of announcement of the federal government's compulsory screen and search order, at up to 100 million dollars per year.[81]

At the time of announcement of its new order, the federal government also indicated that it would fine airports $ 1,000 a day for any failure to comply with the strict new anti-hijacking programme. Four airports, in various parts of the United States, were promptly fined for such failure; though the airport authorities complained that it would require up to 3,500 guards to patrol the nation's 531 airports.[82]

On 15 January 1973, a member of the United States Senate, Senator Vance Hartke of Indiana, pleading his Congressional immunity, refused to submit to a pre-flight search by Delta Airlines at the Indianapolis airport, and was allowed to board the aircraft by the airline's employees.[83] The Federal Aviation Agency (FAA) promptly fined Delta Airlines for its failure to abide by the new federal order, and indicated that it was investigating a similar charge against Allegheny Airlines involving Senator Hartke.[84] On 1 March 1973, it was reported that Senator Hartke had filed a legal suit to force the FAA to stop the airlines from searching the Senator or his property before boarding an aircraft.[85]

---

81. *New York Times,* 10 December 1972.

82. *New York Times,* 10 January 1973.

83. The *Indianapolis Star,* 20 January 1973; *ibid.,* 24 January 1973. Senator Hartke was promptly criticised by other members of the Senate. Senator Barry Goldwater, 1964 Republican Presidential candidate, said that Senators should —"go out of their way to set a good example for the remainder of the public. Senator Hartke's refusal to be searched certainly did nothing to advance the cause of safety in air travel"; the *Indianapolis Star,* 30 January 1973. Senator Marlow Cook (Republican, Kentucky) said—"the politics of the issue be damned—it's just good citizenship" (to submit to airport searches): the *Indianapolis Star,* 8 February 1973.

84. Delta Airlines was reported as having been fined $ 2,000 for allowing Senator Hartke to board the aircraft without a search of his person or baggage; the *New York Times,* 3 February 1973. Delta Airlines later announced that it would pay the fine under protest; the *Indianapolis Star,* 25 April 1973.

85. Senator Hartke, in his legal suit for a declaratory judgment, asserted that the airport search was a "restraint tantamount to temporary arrest and is

The airport authorities for their part, managed, on 5 February 1973, to persuade a federal District Judge in Washington, D.C., to give them a temporary restraining order blocking, for 10 days, the implementation of the Presidential order requiring armed local law enforcement officials to be stationed at airline boarding gates before all commercial flights.[86] All these legal manœuvres were designed to force some settlement of the as yet unresolved question of who should bear the extra financial burden; and this was finally resolved by mid-March 1973, with the announcement that the Civil Aeronautics Board (CAB) had, in effect, approved the passing on of that burden—now revalued downwards to amount to some $ 57.6 million dollars annually—to the general public through the medium of an extra charge of 34 cents to be added to the cost of each airline ticket issued in the United States. The actual premium of 34 cents was approved on an interim basis—subject to revision after more thorough investigation; but the principle of assumption of the burden by the general public was clearly established.[87]

It should be mentioned that the search procedures—both those introduced by the airlines on their own initiative even before the new federal order for compulsory screen and search came into effect, and those introduced as a direct result of the new federal order—have begun to be litigated extensively in the courts, not so much by persons who (like Senator Hartke) may view any search as an infringement of their civil liberties, but, much more, by criminal delinquents who are quite unrelated to any planned hijacking attempt but who are revealed, as a result of anti-hijacking screenings and searches, on the ground, to be carrying various material—for example, narcotics—with would, if constitutionally admissible, be evidence upon which they could be prosecuted for federal or state crimes unrelated to hijacking. The constitutional issue is whether such evidence—be it narcotics, obscene literature, or similar material unrelated to hijacking—when it is turned up in the course of routine anti-hijacking screenings and searches of passengers and their luggage—should be constitutionally admissible in subsequent criminal prosecutions directly based upon such evidence.

---

violative of the very substance and meaning of the privileges and immunities provided for members of the United States Congress in Article One of the Constitution". The *Indianapolis Star,* 1 March 1973.

86. The *New York Times,* 6 February 1973; *ibid.,* 7 February 1973; *ibid.,* 11 February 1973.

87. The *New York Times,* 15 March 1973.

Those who object to the admission of such evidence argue that it violates the US Constitution's Fourth Amendment guarantee against unreasonable searches and seizures.[88] The constitutional debate has also centred around the issue of whether the security officers administering anti-hijacking screenings and searches are constitutionally obligated to give appropriate warning to passengers that they are not obliged to take the searches but that they may elect, instead, not to board the aircraft. This debate takes us, of course, into basic questions of American constitutional law involving, in part, the so-called "Law and Order" theme of the last Presidential election campaign and the often-repeated public charge that US federal courts were showing an excessive deference to claimed civil liberties of accused criminals at the practical expense of the safety of ordinary citizens—what one critic labels as "techno-urban Fascism."[89] It seems likely, however, that as with past constitutional issues, a satisfactory balancing or reconciliation of the competing interests in public security and individual liberties involved in the anti-hijacking control-measures, can be worked out by the US Supreme Court and US federal courts generally in the concrete fact-settings of particular cases:[90] the issue is very complex

88. *Supra,* Chapter 2, footnote 15.

89. "To the many absurd and prevalent apprehensions about the state of civil liberties in the United States, we can now add another: searching air travellers may be a violation of the Fourth Amendment guarantee against unreasonable searches and seizures."

"My concern is to scotch this meaningless fear before it becomes another example to prove America's swift decline into what Professor Bertram Gross would call 'techno-urban fascism'." Arnold Beichman, "Whose Rights?", the *New York Times,* 15 December 1972.

90. The court decisions have, however, up to date tended to be decided by the federal courts *against* the prosecution authorities. See, for example, *U.S.* v. *Lopez,* 328 F. Supp. 1077 (1971) (E.D. N.Y.), where Federal District Court Judge Weinstein allowed defendant's motion to exclude, in a federal criminal prosecution for concealment and facilitating the transportation of narcotic drugs, a tinfoil covered plastic envelope, 4 inches wide and 6 inches long and 3/4 inch thick and tightly packed with heroin, which had been detected in pre-flight boarding inspection involving an electronic magnetometer surveillance and subsequent body search of the defendant who was travelling under a false name. Judge Weinstein held that certain aspects of the pre-flight boarding inspection violated the US Constitution "equal protection" clause and the guarantee against "ureasonable searches and seizures".

On the other hand, in *U.S.* v. *Bell,* 464 F.2d 667 (1972), the United States Court of Appeals for the Second Circuit upheld, against Fourth Amendment ("unreasonable searches and seizures") objections, the criminal conviction of a defendant on evidence (600 glassine envelopes containing heroin) discovered upon his person during pre-flight boarding (magnetometer and body search)

and needs, perhaps, the trial-and-error judicial experimentation of a group of cases, before any really definitive balancing of the conflicting social interests can be arrived at with complete confidence.[91]

The problem is not, of course, limited to the United States. Similar anti-hijacking control screen and search measures, applied by Swedish police authorities at the Gothenburg Airport, in October 1972, to a Swiss banker, Hentsch, about to board an aircraft to Copenhagen, revealed that the Swiss citizen had 11,000 Swedish Kroner in his hand-luggage, and a further 451,200 Swedish Kroner and 23,900 Norwegian Kroner in his remaining luggage—where the legal export limit from Sweden was only 6,000 Swedish Kroner: criminal prosecution of the Swiss banker, Hentsch, for illegal currency smuggling brought a sentence of 4-months' imprisonment, a 5-year ban on any return visit to Sweden, and confiscation of all smuggled currency, though the conviction is now on appeal.[92]

The US Presidential order for screenings and searches at airports does allow for exemption of foreign diplomats and for high US Government officials; but foreign nationals are clearly subject to the controls if they wish to board airliners. It is interesting to note that the statistics as to arrests of travellers at US airports, after the application of on-the-ground, pre-flight, security screenings and searches of passengers and their luggage, indicate that in a period of 20 months to late 1972 more than 6,000 travellers had been arrested, but that fewer than 20 per cent. of these arrests had been for carrying a weapon, or

---

screening of passengers. The defendant at the time of boarding the flight, was already out on bail on other, attempted murder and narcotics, charges. However, in *U.S.* v. *Meulener,* 351 F.Supp. 1284 (1972), Federal District Judge Ferguson of the Central District of California upheld a defence motion in a criminal trial for exclusion, on Fourth Amendment ("unreasonable searches and seizures") grounds, of narcotic drugs found in defendant's carry-on luggage and on his person during pre-flight boarding (magnetometer and body search) screening of passengers. Judge Ferguson held that the search of the defendant's suitcase after the magnetometer had registered positively was constitutionally impermissible because the defendant was not given the opportunity to decline to submit to the search on condition that he not board the aircraft; and alternatively, because an initial pat-down was not made of the defendant's outer clothing for the metal object responsible for the positive magnetometer reading.

91. Though it is important, here, to remember Mr. Justice Felix Frankfurter's admonition as to the limits of the case/controversy approach to community problem-solving: "Only fragments of a social problem are seen through the narrow windows of a litigation." Per Frankfurter J. (dissenting), *Sherrer* v. *Sherrer,* 334 U.S. 343 (1948).

92. *Der Spiegel* (Hamburg), 12 March 1973.

threatening to hijack an airliner, or other charges related to hijacking. More than 2,000 of the travellers were arrested for illegal possession of drugs found when they were searched; with approximately the same number arrested for the offence of illegal entry into the United States, and with the remainder arrested on charges ranging from parole violation to forgery. The American Civil Liberties Union, commenting on these surprising statistics, appeared to believe that federal agents had searched passengers under the pretext of looking for concealed weapons when actually they suspected the passengers of carrying drugs or other contraband.[93]

(ii) Direct action: "sky marshals" and the application of force

Another aspect of preventive control of hijacking through police measures concerns the development of special police or security agents with sharp-shooting experience, designed to be available at short notice on the ground, and usually in disguise, so as to enable concentrated action on the ground against a would-be hijacker. Other plans call for placing such special police or security guards on regular airline flights, in disguise so as to blend easily with other passengers,—the so-called "sky marshals".

The cost of any such measures, especially where it involves putting such special security officials on commercial airline flights on a regular or systematic basis, will no doubt tend to be almost prohibitive. Again, there is a certain amount of scepticism as to the practical results likely to be obtained, on a balance of pains and gains approach: the complete ineptness of the Munich city police sharp-shooters, in the Munich Olympic Games Terrorist kidnapping shoot-out of September 1972, has, perhaps unwarrantedly, brought a general discredit against such "direct action" methods, even when applied on the ground. In the air, the disguised security officer, in trying to apprehend a hijacker, brings, even more than on the ground, the risk of creating a carnival shooting gallery at an altitude of 30,000 feet or more and in a pressurised aircraft cabin. El Al's experience with the airborne security officers who apparently travel on each commercial flight, has been uniformly successful. On the other hand, a US experience on 5 July 1972, where the FBI marshals thwarted an attempted hijacking of a Pacific Southwest Boeing 737 at San Francisco with 86 passengers

93. The *New York Times*, 26 November 1972.

aboard, by killing the two hijackers, was criticised by some because a passenger was also killed in the cross-fire between the FBI officers and the hijackers.[94]

At almost the same time, in July 1972, a Pan American pilot and a passenger managed to foil an attempt to hijack a Pan American plane with 147 persons aboard from Saigon to North Vietnam, the pilot seizing the hijacker by the throat and the passenger managing to kill him. The pilot justified his action of helping to kill the hijacker by pointing out that it was not just an ordinary case of hijacking, since of course the Vietnam War was at its height, and the commercial passenger aircraft also had some US military personnel among its passengers; and they and the passengers would have run the risk of being held as hostages in North Vietnam after landing. On his return to the United States, the pilot received some insulting and threatening letters; and the *New York Times* raised the question: "When may a hijacker be lawfully killed?"[95] In a further discussion entitled, "Who should make the critical decisions?", the *New York Times* pointed to the dangers of a confusion of authority and command structure in regard to planning on-the-spot direct action against hijackers, in criticising the action of FBI agents on the ground in shooting out the main tyres of a hijacked Southern Airways jet just before it was taking off from Orlando, Florida, on the ninth and final leg of one of the most harrowing acts of aerial piracy on record.[96] The pilots, who claimed the ground action was foolhardy, contended that they alone should make the final decision on any application of direct action to control hijackings: the FBI officials argued that it was a decision to be made jointly between the ground security officers and the airline company officials.[97]

---

94. "The FBI's plan was 'well-thought out' ", said J. Floyd Andrews, President of Pacific Southwest, "and it is obvious to me it would have succeeded except for the one hijacker going berserk".

"But some airline executives were not so sure. One called the San Francisco shootout, 'preposterous, a total disaster'. And he said that escalation of force in dealing with skyjackers would only lead to escalation in violence by skyjackers." The *New York Times,* 9 July 1972. On the other hand, as the *New York Times* commented, in its Editorial, "Safety First", published on the same date, the hijackers were threatening to take 79 passengers as well as 5 crewmen with them—"on a hazardous flight to the Soviet Union in an inadequate aircraft in bad weather". *Ibid.*

95. "Shootings of Air Hijackers raise key legal question." The *New York Times,* 10 July 1972.

96. The *New York Times,* 19 November 1972.

97. *Ibid.*

6. *Individual Action: Legal Action by the Individual Passenger*

The individual passenger on a commercial passenger aircraft is really the "forgotten man" in the current debate over hijacking control measures. Airline pilots, as a well-organised professional skill group, can no doubt at least build in to their contractual salary demands extra premiums ("danger money") to take account of the hazards to life and limb and mental well-being posed by the hijacking problem. Airline companies, for their part, can trade-off the mathematical chances of a hijacking against their need not to offend too much, by airflight boycott or other sanctions measures, countries on whose goodwill they depend for obtaining or renewing choice legal landing rights or even for exercising aerial overflight privileges. And governments, weighing the nuisance, in terms both of national prestige and also the tranquil operation of national commercial airline service, constituted by hijackings, can always trade off some potentially quite effective control measures directed against delinquent countries that harbour or protect or otherwise sponsor hijackers, against the need to maintain friendly relations with those countries who may be useful or vital to them for military-strategic, diplomatic, or general commercial reasons.

The individual passenger, by contrast, must sometimes feel that he is the innocent victim of international power plays between nations, or of the selfish pursuit of purely commercial considerations on the part of the airline companies. The individual passenger has no legal standing to sue in international jurisdictions like the International Court of Justice; and no political competence to initiate action before the UN Security Council or General Assembly, or in the ICAO Council or Assembly; and absolutely no presence in the IATA gatherings. He can, perhaps, if he is an individual shareholder of a national commercial airline company, try to take the difficult legal path of launching a private stockholder's suit or even asking awkward questions at the company's annual meeting, in order to try to compel more sustained and effective anti-hijacking initiatives on the part of his company and its directors, within its own sphere of operations and also in international reunions like those of IATA.

By and large, however, the passenger is left to all the difficulties and time delays of a private legal action against the airline company that originally contracted to carry him and his luggage safely to his designated destination. Arising out of Tel Aviv's Lydda airport massacre of 30 May 1972, perpetrated by a three-man Japanese suicide squad who had been instructed by Palestine Terrorist groups, the survivors and families of a group of Puerto Rican Christian pilgrims, who had arrived in Israel on the same Air France flight as the criminal assassins, filed suits in the US District Court in San Juan, Puerto Rico, against Air France on behalf of 86 plaintiffs in 10 separate claims. The suits, which claimed a total of 11 million dollars, sought compensation for actual injuries sustained, mental anguish, medical treatment, and loss of income: the suits alleged that Air France failed properly to screen the passengers who boarded the Air France plane at Rome's Fiumicino airport where the three Japanese gunmen embarked. Air France, in reply, contended that it was not legally responsible for injuries suffered by its passengers at the Tel Aviv airport because they had crossed a police check-point and were out of the company's hands.[98]

A United States District Court (for the Southern District of New York) has had occasion to rule, in *Husserl* v. *Swiss Air Transport Company, Ltd.*,[99] on individual passenger civil claims arising from the Palestine Terrorist organisation's mass hijacking of aircraft to the Jordanian desert in September 1970. The plaintiff, a New York resident, had been a passenger on a Swiss Air aircraft scheduled for a direct flight from Zurich to New York on 6 September 1970, and she raised three causes of action: first, a claim under the Warsaw Convention of 1929, as modified by the so-called Montreal Agreement of 1966; second, a claim in breach of contract for safe carriage to New York; and third, a claim for injuries based on the alleged negligence of the defendant Swiss Air company or that of its agents. Exercising jurisdiction on a basis of the diversity of citizenship of the parties, the US federal District Court rejected a Swiss Air company defence to the effect that the plaintiff passenger's first claim under the Warsaw Convention was not an "accident" within the intendment of Article 17 of that Convention and therefore not sufficient to raise the presumption of liability under that Convention as modified by the Montreal Agreement. In reaching this conclusion, the federal District Court judge, Judge Tyler, relied strongly upon Article 31 (3) (6) of the Vienna Convention on the Law of Treaties of 1969, allowing the subsequent action of parties to a treaty (here principally the

98. *International Herald Tribune* (Paris), 22 August 1972.
99. 351 F. Supp. 702 (1972).

action as to the so-called Montreal Agreement) to be taken into account as a prime canon of treaty construction in respect to the interpretation of the Warsaw Convention, in areas clearly unanticipated at the time of its original drafting and signing. In finding that the Montreal Agreement imposed a system of "absolute liability" upon the defendant air carrier, Judge Tyler took note of the fact that—

> "the Montreal liability system is based on a combination of treaty, contract, and administrative approval, and since it was hammered out by the State Department with the active support of the Civil Aeronautics Board and the Federal Aviation Agency, its 'legislative history' may include the public expressions of the State Department and the Civil Aeronautics Board."[100]

Having so found against the defendant Swiss Air company on the first, of Warsaw Convention, count, the US District Court found it unnecessary to rule upon the plaintiff passenger's remaining two counts.[101] The case is now on appeal to the United States Court of Appeals for the Second Circuit.

There remain, even after this first decision by a US federal court on the matter of the airline company's civil liability in damages to a passenger in a hijacked aircraft, a number of interesting and as yet not finally litigated questions going to insurance and related liability questions. Are, for example, insurance companies that contract to insure airline companies in respect to their commercial passenger operations legally bound, under those insurance contracts, to indemnify the airline companies against claims or losses arising from hijackings—both individual passengers' claims in contract or delict against the company, and also the airline companies' own losses arising from destruction or damage to the hijacked aircraft and the disruption of the companies' normal commercial operations. While such questions, as between insurance company and airline company, must obviously turn on the particular contracts of insurance involved, it may be affected

100. *Per* Tyler J., 351 F. Supp. 702, at p. 706 (1972); citing L. Kreindler, *Aviation Accident Law* (1971), s. 12A. 02 at 3. And see also Sir William Hildred, "Air Carriers' Liability: Significance of the Warsaw Convention and Events Leading up to the Montreal Agreement", *Journal of Air Law and Commerce*, Vol. 33 (1967), p. 521; R. H. Mankiewicz, "Le statut de l'arrangement de Montréal (mai 1966) et la décision du Civil Aeronautics Board du 13 mei 1966 concernant la responsabilité de certains transporteurs aériens a l'égard de leurs passagers", *Revue française de droit aérien* (1967), p. 1.

101. *Ibid.*, at p. 707.

by the existence or otherwise in the contract of special "war risk" exclusion clauses.[102] In this regard, however, even if the insurance contract should positively and in terms exclude "war risks" it is open to argument whether the various activities of the Palestinian National Liberation Front and other Palestine terrorist groups should be regarded as "war" operations. These Palestine nationalist groups themselves make claim, from time to time, to a special international law status of "irregular", "privileged combatancy"; but these particular groups have so far not been accorded any governmental status, *de jure* or *de facto,* and they therefore as yet can hardly be brought within the traditional doctrines of State responsibility.[103] This again, however, is a matter that must turn on the particular insurance contracts: it is a matter that is being much discussed at present between insurance and airline companies' lawyers, following on the major financial losses stemming from the September 1970 hijackings to the Jordanian desert with the resultant total destruction of the aircraft involved; but so far no actual litigation thereon has been reported.

---

102. See, generally, "Versicherungs- und Haftungs-Fragen bei Luftpiraterie", in A. Meyer, *Internationale Luftfahrtabkommen* (1972), pp. 220-234.

More generally, as to Conflicts of Laws (Private International Law) questions, and particularly jurisdictional and choice of law issues, involved in such litigation, which will usually, because involving international flights, have multi-State elements in the problem fact-situation, see L. M. Bentivoglio, "Conflicts Problems in Air Law", *Recueil des cours de l'Académie de droit international de La Haye* (1966), III, p. 75.

103. See, in this regard, the detailed Comments by Madame Bastid in response to the *Provisional Report* of the Institut de Droit International's Eighteenth Commission ("Hijacking of Aircraft"), *Annuaire de l'Institut de droit international,* Vol. 54, I (1971), pp. 520 *et seq.*

CHAPTER 4

THE OBJECTIVES OF INTERNATIONAL LEGAL PROBLEM-SOLVING IN REGARD TO AERIAL HIJACKING: THE MAIN ALTERNATIVE WORLD COMMUNITY OPTIONS AND THEIR MACHINERY-INSTRUMENTAL BASES

The difficulties in arriving at firm agreement on the best techniques for international legal problem-solving in regard to aerial hijacking are only partly to be explained by the inherent difficulties of a problem that is rooted in the conflicts and contradictions, already referred to, of the contemporary, technologically based, post-industrial, "Western" or at least "Westernised", society. A good deal of the failure to arrive at practical solutions for the problem stems from failure, in international legal arenas, properly to define the problem itself or at least to arrive at a minimum working consensus of its nature and incidents. While some of the blame for this can no doubt be attributed to cloudy thinking on the part of international diplomats who may too often be prepared to sacrifice clarity of thought to the oratorical pleasures of talking at length or taking cheap debating points against political opponents, the basic explanation seems to be rather in political timorousness on the part of individual national delegations in refusing honestly to explain their own particular national objectives in regard to the hijacking problem. This lack of clarity and candour as to national objectives has impeded the scientific identification of the range of competing community interests present in the problem-situation; and impeded, therefore, the establishment of a scientific scheme of such interests, involving some form of appraisal or quantification of the varying social weight of such interests and the social cost—based on the balance of pains and gains—involved in giving effect to them. For, in fact, no one, single societal interest is involved in the aerial hijacking problem-situation, but a plethora of different and sometimes directly competing societal interests; and the process of rational community decision-making involves, therefore, some sort of conscious community choice or preference exercised between those different social interests in concrete cases. What this involves, ultimately, in order to obtain an over-all, World Community consensus on a desirable solution or solutions to the hijacking problem, is a genuine, and not simply verbal, consensus as to the hierarchy of values or policies involved in solution.

While all States may be committed to the principle of the "freedom of the air",—meaning, here, the safety and regularity of air transport and communications—in the abstract, it is apparent that, in the concrete, their degrees of deference to that principle will vary widely, depending in part on the particular modalities of its application in particular cases, and on the other, counter-vailing principles present in the same cases. Thus, though the United States and Cuba will both accept the principle of the "freedom of the air", in terms of their political confrontation over the decade of the 1960s in the rash of "Cuban" hijackings, neither State, clearly, was prepared to base itself 100 per cent. on that principle. The United States, given the evident practical option in the early 1960s of a firm, formal agreement with Cuba on compulsory rendition of hijackers to the country of their crime, preferred no formal agreement at all with Cuba; since the price, or *quid pro quo,* involved, logically, reciprocal US obligations to return to Cuba anti-Castro refugees who had hijacked ships or aircraft as a means of escaping from Cuba. The United States, in this instance, itself balanced, or, if you wish, off-set or down-graded somewhat the principle of the "freedom of the air" by deference to the (in American terms) historically well-regarded principle of political asylum (and freedom from compulsory extradition to their homeland) of *bona fide* political actors. Cuba, for its part, balanced its own deference, such as it might be, to the principle of the "freedom of the air", against its obvious opportunities to maximise the inconvenience and embarrassment caused to the United States by the rash of "Cuban" hijackings and so to try to force a political settlement with the United States ending Cuba's effective political and economic isolation in the Western Hemisphere. As the political irritation to the United States mounted in pace with the acceleration in the frequency and the gravity of the hijackings to Cuba, so did the dangers to Cuba of becoming known as a "haven" for hijackers, the overwhelming majority of whom turned out to be, in the case of Cuba, mentally deranged or unbalanced individuals or common criminals,—without any colour of *bona fide* political motivation. Everything pointed, therefore, to the US-Cuban "pragmatic compromise" as to control and practical alleviation of the consequences of hijackings, which persisted successfully over the 1960s until formally ratified and completed in the US-Cuban Memorandum of Understanding of February 1973, already discussed.

In the case of the Middle Eastern hijackings, the clear difference in basic national attitudes as to the relative degree of priority or preference to be given to the different competing interests; the difference, further, even as to those interests that should properly be taken into account and so recognised in constructing any scientific scheme of interests; and, finally, the difference even as to the definition of the nature of the problem itself [1] shine through the long-winded,

---

1. The intellectual conflicts as to basic legal characterization of the problem itself, manifest in the hijacking control debates, are even more marked in the cognate area of legal control of international terrorism. See, in this regard, the resolution adopted by the UN General Assembly on 18 December 1972, on measures to prevent international terrorism. The resolution—picturesquely entitled—

> "Measures to prevent international terrorism which endangers or takes innocent human lives or jeopardises fundamental freedoms, and study of the underlying causes of those forms of terrorism and acts of violence which lie in misery, frustration, grievance and despair and which cause some people to sacrifice human lives, including their own, in an attempt to effect radical changes"—

was adopted by the UN General Assembly by a vote of 76 in favour (mainly the Afro-Asian and Soviet bloc countries); 35 against (mainly the Western European, North American, and Latin American countries); with 17 abstentions (including France and Sweden). *United Nations, Weekly News Summary,* 22 December 1972.

Resolution 3034 (XXVII), 18 December 1972. The vote on the measure sponsored by Algeria was widely interpreted as a vote to shelve, or at least postpone, action on legal control of international terrorism since, apart from expressing "deep perturb(ation)" and "deep concern", the substance of the resolution was essentially to call for "study" of the problem. Two alternative proposals, both rendered abortive by the adoption of the Algerian proposal, involved respectively a US plan to convene an international conference in 1973 with powers to draw up a convention on terrorism—see in this regard USA: working paper, Draft Convention for the Prevention and Punishment of certain acts of international terrorism (UN Doc. A/C.6/L.850, 25 September 1972); *International Legal Materials,* Vol. 11 (November 1972), p. 1382; and a "compromise" British formula calling on the International Law Commission to draft, "with highest priority", a convention on hijacking to be submitted to a plenipotentiary conference at the earliest possible date, and also calling for a study committee to look into underlying causes of terrorism. And see also the International Law Commission's Draft Articles on the Prevention and Punishment of Crimes against diplomatic agents and other internationally protected persons (Report of the I.L.C. on the Work of its Twenty-fourth Session (2 May-7 July 1972), UN Doc. A/8710, 22 July 1972; reproduced in *International Legal Materials,* Vol. 11 (September 1972), p. 977), follow-up action on which has been markedly lacking. See address by US Secretary of State, William P. Rogers, to UN General Assembly, 25 September 1972; *United Nations Law Reports,* Vol. 7 [1 October 1972].

rambling, and repetitive debates in international legal arenas.[2]

The adoption of the Algerian "study" proposal on 18 December 1972, and consequent burying of the US and the British hard-line measures, was described as a "stunning defeat for strong international legal action against terrorism", *New York Times,* 21 December 1972; a "direct rebuff to the forthright leadership of Secretary-General Kurt Waldheim, who saw the dangers of terrorism as precisely the kind of issue on which the UN could reassert some responsibility for world security",—"U.N. Defaults", *ibid.,* 13 December 1972; "cutting through the purposefully dense diplomatic verbiage, it appeared to Western representatives that the resolution could be interpreted as encouraging terrorists to do their worst so long as their efforts were aimed at self-determination of their people",—"United Nations, Hands Off on issue of Terror", *ibid.,* 17 December 1972.

2. In the debate in the UN General Assembly, on legal control of international terrorism, the Chinese delegate, Pi Chi-lung, condemned acts of terrorism, but defended the "just struggles" of the African liberation movements and the Palestinians, insisting that they were "not terrorism at all"; *New York Times,* 22 November 1972. The Chinese indicated that they opposed inclusion of the item in the agenda and considered that the type of terrorism perpetrated by the few individuals "divorced from the masses" was a matter within the jurisdiction of the country in which the acts occurred. *United Nations, Weekly News Summary,* 24 November 1972.

The Iraqi delegate, Professor Mustafa K. Yasseen, in urging the UN to "move cautiously and exercise patience", reminded the UN General Assembly that the old League of Nations had spent three years on a convention against terrorism, which never came into force. *New York Times,* 17 November 1972.

As to earlier era, international action, and especially the abortive League of Nations attempts to counter international terrorism, involving the two 1937 Conventions,—for the Prevention of Terrorism and for the creation of an International Criminal Court—action spurred particularly by the assassination of King Alexander of Yugoslavia and French Foreign Minister Barthou, in 1934—see V. V. Pella, "La répression des crimes contre la personnalité de l'état", *Recueil des cours de l'Académie de droit international de La Haye* (1930), III, p. 677; A. Sottile, "Le terrorisme international", *Recueil des cours de l'Académie de droit international de La Haye* (1938), III, p. 91; H. Donnedieu de Vabres, "La répression internationale du terrorisme. Les Conventions de Genève (16 novembre 1937)", *Revue de droit international et de législation comparée* (3rd Series, Vol. 19 (1938)), p. 37; C. Eustathiades, "La cour pénale internationale pour la répression du terrorisme et le problème de la responsabilité internationale des Etats", *Revue générale de droit international public,* Vol. 43 (1936), p. 385; A. von Gretshaninow, "Der Plan eines internationalen Abkommens betreffend die Bekämpfung politischen Verbrechen un die Errichtung eines internationalen Strafgerichtshofs", *Zeitschrift für ausländisches öffentliches Recht und Völkerrecht,* Vol. 5 (1935), p. 181; H. Mosler, "Die Konferenz zur internationalen Bekämpfung des Terrorismus (November 1937)", *Zeitschrift für ausländisches öffentliches Recht und Völkerrecht,* Vol. 8 (1938), p. 99; *Annuaire de l'Institut de droit international,* Vol. 54 (I) (1971), pp. 520 *et seq.*; A. H. Kuhn, "The Complaint of Yugoslavia against Hungary with Reference to the Assassination of King Alexander", *American Journal of International Law,* Vol. 29 (1935), p. 87; M. Liais, "L'affaire hungaro-yougoslave devant le conseil de la société des nations", *Revue générale de droit international public,* Vol.

Stated in very clear terms, for some States' delegates, the Middle Eastern hijackings represent a quite intolerable—and, in their actual circumstances, viciously cruel and inhuman—interference with the security of international communications. For some other States, however, the Middle Eastern hijackers are simply trying to vindicate, by perhaps unusual and unorthodox methods, legitimate principles of international law, and particularly the principles of the so-called "new" international law—which, it is claimed, they are unable to express in more normal or traditionally licit ways through the existence of effective clogs on the processes of international legal change. The unbridgeable gap, in contemporary terms, between these two basic legal characterisations of the same concrete problem-situation—the freedom of the air *versus* national self-determination—explains the general failure to secure multilateral conventions, in control of hijacking, that really do have some teeth in them but that are capable, nevertheless, of universal or near universal signature and ratification.

The gap between these two basic characterisations of the problem-situation does not, however, altogether explain the failure of leading "airline" States, that do have the effective power,—by denial of national landing rights, for example,—to inflict real economic deprivations on delinquent States, to follow through with their own nationally based, and preferably "regional", sanctions programmes in order to vindicate the principle of the "freedom of the air". The inference must be that these States themselves accept that the dichotomy,—freedom of the air *versus* national self-determination,—is formulated in too absolutistic and black-and-white terms, and that the characterisation of the problem and therefore its solution in concrete cases needs to be properly nuanced so as to take note of the particular facts of those cases. Of course, as an additional element, many leading "airline" States are necessarily influenced, in their political attitudes to the Middle Eastern hijackings, by the fact that they are themselves heavily dependent on Middle Eastern countries both for important regional, aerial landing or overflight facilities and, much more importantly, for oil supplies for national defence and economic purposes.

In the main Western countries, the traditions of political liberty and freedom of political expression have imposed important limitations on control of aerial hijacking, so far as that may be thought to involve

---

42 (1935), p. 127; H. von Weber, "Terrorismus", in Strupp-Schlochauer (editors), *Wörterbuch des Völkerrechts* (Vol. 3) (1962), p. 439.

compulsory extradition to the country of nationality of the hijacker or to the country on whose airline the hijacking was committed. What a Swedish writer calls "the moralising tendency found today in a number of Western countries and particularly in Sweden ... [that] is likely to oppose every country pursuing a policy not satisfying local demand", may end up, as a practical matter, that "an enemy of a nation unfriendly with Sweden is certain to find sanctuary in Sweden".[3] In the actual jurisprudence, countries like Sweden, Switzerland, France, Austria, Greece, West Germany, Denmark, Italy, have persistently refused to consider extraditing hijackers where there is clear, or even colourable, evidence of a "political" motive for the hijacking. These countries have preferred, instead—rendering lip service at least to the principle *aut dedere, aut punire*—to try the hijackers before their own national criminal courts, the sentences generally being, because of the "political" element, very light, or even nominal to the point of being absurd.[4] The claimed "political" motives recognised by these Western national courts run the whole gamut of political causes and political ideologies: France (Italian nationals hijacking Greek plane because of claimed opposition to Greek Government); France (Polish nationals hijacking Polish airliner to French sector of West Berlin); Austria (Polish nationals hijacking Polish airliner); Greece (Palestinians hijacking American TWA aircraft); Sweden (Greek national hijacking Greek Olympic Airways aircraft to Cairo); Sweden (Greek hijacking Greek Olympic Airways aircraft to Albania); Sweden (Colombian national hijacking Colombian aircraft to Cuba); West Germany (Czech national hijacking Czech plane to West Germany); Denmark (Polish national hijacking Polish airliner to Denmark); Italy (Italian-born naturalised American citizen hijacking American TWA aircraft to Rome).[5] Sometimes, as in the last-mentioned

3. J. W. F. Sundberg, "The Case for an International Criminal Court", *Journal of Air Law and Commerce,* Vol. 37 (1971), p. 211, at p. 221.

4. France in 1969 imposed sentences of five months and eight months imprisonment respectively on two Italian nationals who claimed "political" motives for hijacking a Greek Olympic Airways aircraft and forcing it to return to Orly airport in Paris. *Revue générale de l'Air et de l'Espace* (1969), p. 358; Sundberg, *op. cit.,* at pp. 217-218.

5. Sundberg, *op. cit.,* at p. 218; Sundberg, "'Abu Thalaat', la guerre contre l'aviation civile internationale", *Revue française de droit aérien* (1972 (No. 2)), p. 1; *Revue de droit pénal et de criminologie* (October 1971). And see generally, W. H. Reeves, "Political Hijacking: What Law applies in Peace and War", *Vanderbilt Law Review,* Vol. 22 (1969), p. 1117; Y. Pimon, "La subversion dans les relations internationales contemporaines", *Revue générale de droit international public* (1972), p. 768.

Italian case, the Western asylum country may become sorely embarrassed and look ridiculous in terms of the operation of its national judicial processes: the Italian-American, Minichiello, after being greeted as a sort of folk hero in Italy with Carlo Ponti talking of making a film out of his hijacking exploit, was sentenced to 7½ years imprisonment by an Italian court in 1970, but then quietly released after serving only a few months of his sentence—to go on a chequered history of inability to hold steady employment and repeated minor brushes with the law.[6] Beyond that, however, it is recorded that since (and presumably in direct reaction to) the Jordanian desert hijackings of September 1970, there has been a trend to much heavier sentencing on the part of Western courts that are themselves trying the cases of hijackers.

Perhaps the most important jurisprudential principle in these Western court decisions—all of which proceed on the principle *aut dedere, aut punire,* and (accepting the claimed "political" element in those cases) accept also the concomitant obligation to punish under one's own legal system in *lieu* of any extradition—is the one emerging from the first decision of all, the decision rendered in 1952 by the Federal Supreme Court of Switzerland.[7] In that case, the Swiss court had to rule directly on a request for extradition made by the Yugoslav Government, under the Swiss-Serbian Extradition Treaty, in regard to Yugoslav nationals who had hijacked a Yugoslav airliner to Zurich. The Swiss Supreme Court attempted, in its decision on the extradition issue, to elaborate principles to govern the "political exception" to extradition proceedings; and it focussed directly upon the question of the relation between ends and means—between the objective of political escape and the measures actually chosen by the hijackers to effectuate that purpose, including necessarily the degree of consideration and respect shown for the interests of other persons (the innocent aircrew and passengers) and any injuries or deprivations inflicted upon such other persons in the process of escape. The Swiss court noted that, under the facts of the case before it, the defendants had no prospect of being able to emigrate with their families legally, having regard to the laws of Yugoslavia which indeed, in the Penal Code, specifically established, under the Chapter "Offences against the People and the

---

6. *Supra,* Chapter 1, footnote 11.

7. Decision of the Federal Supreme Court of Switzerland, 30 April 1952. 78 *Entscheidungen des Bundesgerichts* I, 39 (1952); *International Legal Reports,* Vol. 19 (1952), p. 371.

State", a special offence entitled "Act of fleeing abroad pursuant to hostile activity". In refusing the request for extradition on the part of the Yugoslav Government, the Swiss court found that, on the facts, the defendants had met the test of establishing a certain relationship between the goal of escape and the means of attaining it, so that the ideals associated with the goal were strong enough to excuse, if not to justify, the injury to private juridical interests resulting from the act.[8]

Applied to the mass of subsequent hijackings, effectuated with claimed "political" motives of escape, the Swiss Supreme Court's reasoning might seem to lead to the following principle (assuming, of course, that the claimed "political" motive was in fact found, on examination, to be *bona fide*):

> A hijacker, acting with a political motive, who hijacks a plane as a method of escape from his home country to political asylum, should be exempted from compulsory extradition process if no other alternative method of escape or departure from his home country is reasonably available to him, and if, in the actual execution of the escape, he does not kill or injure or needlessly endanger innocent passengers and air crew in the hijacked aircraft.

Such a formulation would seem to have the advantage of being very close to the present law-in-action as administered by courts actually passing on such cases; and also of striking some sort of reasonable balance between a claimed "new" international law-based "freedom of movement" (or the "right to emigrate") on the one hand,[9] and both the "freedom of the air" and also the private law-based prin-

8. Donnedieu de Vabres stresses this same point as to the procedures or *means* actually employed by the authors of political *attentats* to achieve their political or social goals, citing here the special *clause d'attentat* which, since the Franco-Belgian Convention of 22 March 1856, has penetrated into numerous treaties and which withdraws from the benefit of political asylum and submits to political extradition the assassins of Heads of State. And see also the Resolution of the Institut de Droit International, adopted in Geneva in 1892, which expressly excludes from the category of political delicts—"des crimes les plus graves du point de vue de la morale et du droit commun, tels que l'assassinat, le meutre ...". H. Donnedieu de Vabres, "La répression internationale du terrorisme. Les Conventions de Genève (16 novembre 1937)", *Revue de droit international et de législation comparée* (3rd Series, Vol. 19 (1938)), p. 37, especially at pp. 43-44.

9. *Supra,* Chapter 1, footnote 8, re that "freedom of movement" supposedly guaranteed under general international law.

ciple, stemming from Civil Law and Common Law doctrines as to Abuse of Rights, that any person should so act, in the exercise of his own rights, as not gratuitously to inflict injury upon another person or that other person's rights. The principle of economy in the use of power—in the exercise of private power as well as governmental—and of the necessary reasonable balance between ends and means—is of course at the core of contemporary pragmatic legal philosophy.

CHAPTER 5

THE BALANCE-SHEET OF INTERNATIONAL LEGAL PROBLEM-SOLVING IN REGARD TO AERIAL HIJACKING: HOLISTIC OR GLOBAL SOLUTIONS VERSUS PRAGMATIC, EMPIRICAL, PROBLEM-ORIENTED METHODS

Is it placing too great a burden for salvation upon the "special legal community of the air", to ask it to solve all the great unresolved political *causes célèbres* of the contemporary World Community, either because those problems arise interstitially to an aircraft hijacking, or because (far more often) an aircraft hijacking is the favoured instrument of certain political pressure groups for trying to draw attention to the claimed inherent injustices of those great unresolved *causes célèbres*? The "special legal community of the air", it may be submitted, hardly contains the specialist professional skill-groups best equipped for finding equitable solutions to major tension-issues like the continuing Middle Eastern crisis; or, even more, for ensuring that those solutions really will be politically viable, in the sense of being accepted by the main national governments or *de facto* political movements involved, or, if need be, being actively enforced against them. Even if the "special legal community of the air" were concluded to be adequately equipped to venture upon this sort of major tension-issue problem-solving, it may be questioned whether the relatively narrow contours of an aerial hijacking case provides the best vehicle for World Community examination of the fundamental geopolitical and ideological conflicts (with their inevitable Big Power ramifications), involved in the Middle Eastern crisis and situations of parallel stature. It may be noted, in this regard, that in the case of the earlier, Cold War, East-West hijackings, both the Soviet Bloc and the West, in the era of Bipolarity, resisted any temptations to escalate isolated hijacking incidents, in spite of their Cold War ideological undertones, into Big Power confrontations; just as the United States, facing the mounting irritations of the proliferating "Cuban" hijackings of the 1960s decade, scrupulously avoided any search for a Bay of Pigs-style, "end-solution" and preferred to work out a pragmatic accommodation with Cuba.

There is a striking case for allowing ICAO and IATA and similar specialised international bodies, both inter-governmental and private, to limit themselves to their own "special competence" and so not to try to exceed the air security and safety aspects of hijacking problems coming before them. The other, more generally political aspects of those problems, transcending the air security and safety aspects, belong, it may be argued, to the more general political organs of the World Community, the UN Security Council and General Assembly; or to national governments, acting individually or collectively and regionally in accord with the UN Charter, if the main world peace-keeping organs should fail to fulfil their responsibilities.

Ultimately, to insist that the security or safety of air transport and communications is a paramount interest that must prevail over other, countervailing interests that are sometimes present in concrete hijacking problem-situations—such as claimed, just frontier or general territorial settlements, or even self-determination and independence,—is to assert that the "freedom of the air" should rank today as something in the nature of a super-eminent legal principle or *jus cogens*.[1] To be sure, a very persuasive case can be made that, just as it was, long, long ago, recognised that the immunities of foreign ambassadors or envoys were indispensable to any sort of civilised dialogue between States and thus an indispensable starting point for international law, so security and regularity of transport and communications (by air, sea, or land, or through the mails) are also first principles of international relations—indispensable, as such, to friendly relations and co-operation among States in accord with the UN Charter and *a fortiori* to minimum coexistence between ideologically opposed political

1. As to *jus cogens,* see generally G. Schwarzenberger, "International *Jus Cogens?*", *Texas Law Review,* Vol. 43 (1965), p. 455; A. Verdross, "Forbidden: Treaties in International Law: Comments on Professor Garner's Report on 'The Law of Treaties' ", *American Journal of International Law,* Vol. 31 (1937), p. 571; Verdross, "*Jus dispositivum* and *Jus Cogens* in International Law", *American Journal of International Law,* Vol. 60 (1966), p. 55; M. Virally, "Réflexions sur le *Jus Cogens*", *Annuaire français de droit international* (1966), p. 5; *The Concept of Jus Cogens in International Law. Papers and Proceedings* (Carnegie Endowment for International Peace (European Centre), Geneva (1967)); G. I. Tunkin, "V. I. Lenin i printsipii otnoshenii mezhdu sotsialisticheskimi gosudarstvami" (1969), *Sovetskii Ezhegodnik Mezhdunarodnogo Prava,* p. 19, at p. 28; L. A. Aleksidze, "Problema *Jus Cogens* v sovremennom mezhdunarodnom prave" (1969), *Sovetskii Ezhegodnik Mezhdunarodnogo Prava,* p. 127; I. N. Karpenko, "Imperativnie normi *(Jus Cogens)* i ikh voploshchenie v mezhdunarodnikh dogovorakh" (1970), *Sovetskii Ezhegodnik Mezhdunarodnogo Prava,* p. 204.

systems. Acceptance of any such *jus cogens* character for the "freedom of the air" would imply, quite obviously, that whatever the ultimate rights or wrongs of the great unresolved political struggles of our times and the merits of claims of various political movements, not being States, to "privileged" or "irregular combatancy" status, there would be an absolute bar against resort to hijacking or other crimes of violence against aircraft and their passengers and aircrew, as a means of carrying on such struggles—this under pain of the severest sanctions. It is not necessary to speculate upon the nature of any such ultimate sanctions, which presumably would have to be in the nature at least of the world hue and cry after the 19th-century Barbary pirates;[2] for the World Community, in its prime organised political arenas, the UN Security Council and General Assembly, has shown no real inclination to depart from rhetorical statements of abstract general principles and to venture along the path of concreteness. Nor, of course, have any of the leading "airline" States, in spite of all their legal options to apply what would be, certainly, in respect to at least some States that are well known today as havens for hijackers, highly effective deterrent sanctions. On this empirical evidence, therefore, the "freedom of the air" is certainly not regarded today as an absolute or paramount principle, but a relative one, the degree of whose compromise with other competing interests will be determined only in concrete cases, depending in part on the particular State-participants in those cases.

If we turn away, for the moment, from the search for holistic or global solutions to the hijacking problem, and resolve instead to be pragmatic and operational, it is obvious that hijacking, as a polycentric problem, lends itself to particularisation in terms both of geographical region or area, and also the nature and personality of the individual actors involved.

First of all, the so-called "Cuban" hijackings clearly permitted a viable solution on a bilateral, US-Cuban, "regional" (Caribbean and Western Hemisphere) basis, first in an informal accord that was faithfully observed for over a decade, and then, most recently, in the formal Memorandum of Understanding of February 1973—and this without any help and perhaps only hindrance, from attempts at more gen-

2. The analogy is made by Professor Karl Loewenstein, "Sovereignty in the Skies", *New York Times,* 10 January 1973.

eral or global solutions in multi-nation arenas such as the UN proper, ICAO, and IATA.

As a second example, since only a certain (and minority) percentage of hijacking cases raise genuine "political" elements involving *bona fide* political motivations on the part of the individual actors, the *majority* ("lunatic fringe") hijackings seem readily attuned, in terms of solution, to prompt and effective compulsory extradition of the hijackers to the country of the original crime,—usually, no doubt, for ultimate detention and treatment of the hijacker in a mental institution. Even in the *minority* of cases involving genuine "political" elements, it should be possible to separate off, as being properly subject to compulsory extradition, the cases where the hijacker, even in pursuit of a *bona fide* political objective such as emigration and political asylum, kills or injures innocent persons or acts with wilful disregard for their physical security, in the actual carrying out of the hijacking.

This leaves, then, only the genuine "hard core" politically motivated hijackings; and here the obligation of every State that does not accept the idea of compulsory extradition is, on the *aut dedere, aut punire* basis, to follow through and apply an appropriately severe punishment of the hijacker under its own national criminal laws, under the risk of whatever general obloquy or individual national or regional sanctions—depriving of air landing rights, air traffic boycotts, and the like—that the World Community may apply to a State failing to live up to its obligation, as a "good neighbour",[3] towards other States.[4]

It should not be too difficult to draft effective new international

3. See, in terms of municipal law, Stammler's notional "special community", and the concept that every legal demand can only be maintained in such a way that the person obligated may remain a neighbour (fellow-creature). Stammler, *Lehre von dem richtigen Recht* (1902); and see also Lord Atkin's celebrated opinion enunciating the "neighbour" principle, in *Donoghue* v. *Stevenson,* [1932] A.C. 562, at 580; Constitution of the USSR (1936), Articles 130, 131.

4. At the international law level, the "neighbour" principle is reflected in the *Trail Smelter Arbitration,* 3 *UN Rep. Intl.Arb. Awards 1905* (1949); and see P. Schneider, "Trail Smelter-Fall", in Strupp-Schlochauer (editors), *Wörterbuch des Völkerrechts,* Vol. 3 (1962), p. 447. In the *Corfu Channel Case (Merits)* —*(International Court of Justice,* 1949, *Reports of Judgments,* Judgment of 9 April 1949, at p. 22)—the World Court placed Albania's liability to Great Britain for failure to notify British ships about mines in the Albanian waters of the Corfu Channel, on—"certain general and well-recognised principles", including "every State's obligation not to allow knowingly its territory to be used for acts contrary to the rights of other States". And see generally J. Andrassy, "Les relations internationales de voisinage", *Recueil des cours de l'Académie de droit international de La Haye* (1951), II, p. 77.

control measures on such a basis, particularised in relation to the categories of cases considered.[5] If it is a rather different methodological approach to the pursuit, once again, of some more general and necessarily high-level and abstract, general principles of international law of the sort normally found in the too often unratified—or if ratified, too often ignored—many party, multilateral convention, this essentially pragmatic, empirical, problem-oriented, step-by-step approach to the solution of international hijackings does remind us that the international lawyer's first task is to try to be operational and to do his best to solve a particular problem, even if only on a limited basis.

Of course, it needs emphasising also that it is not the international lawyer's obligation necessarily to try to solve problems that are capable of being solved, or that are better solved, under national law and administration. It is not the World Community's function, for example, to try to decide the ultimate merits of the "Law and Order" theme of the 1972 US Presidential election campaign and the occasional charge that an essentially abstract, un-fact-oriented, "elitist liberal" philosophy [6]—"techno-urban Fascism"—on the part of the US federal

---

5. See, for example, in relation to the obligations contained in Article 11 of the Tokyo Convention of 1963 (State where hijacked aircraft lands to take all appropriate steps to restore control of aircraft to its lawful commander, and to permit passengers and crew to continue their journey as soon as practicable) (Chapter 3, *1, (a), supra*), K. Hailbronner, "Entführte Flugzeuge auf fremden Staatsgebiet und die analoge Anwendung Humanitärer Grundsätze im Völkerrecht", *Zeitschrift für ausländisches öffentliches Recht und Völkerrecht,* Vol. 32 (1972), p. 265; and see also Hailbronner, *Der Schutz der Luftgrenzen im Frieden* (1972), especially at p. 23 as to the obligation of the ground State to help an aircraft in distress. And see generally O. Lissitzyn, "The Treatment of Aerial Intruders in Recent Practice and International Law", *American Journal of International Law,* Vol. 47 (1953), p. 559; Resolution of the *Institut de Droit International,* on Unlawful Diversion of Aircraft, adopted at the Zagreb Session on 3 September 1971—*Annuaire de l'Institut de Droit International,* Vol. 54 (1971).

6. "Legislation to cure slum problems has tended to be written not by politicians with black constituencies but by politicians with upper-middle-class reformer constituencies. This means legislation that provides money not to hire lower-middle-class policemen, but money to hire upper-middle-class social workers and lawyers to implement upper-middle-class 'solutions'. No one has bothered to ask the folks in Harlem whether they would rather have Uncle Sam buy them a poverty war or lock up the drug addicts.

In fact, what could improve life in the slums faster than a sharp reduction in the drug problem? Yet upper-middle-class sensibilities work not for such a step but against it. When *your* neigbourhood and *your* children are not affected, it is much easier to take the view that an addict is sick, not a criminal. Also, middle-class reformers often carry an animus against law enforcement in general.

judiciary and law enforcement establishment in general,—may have so hamstrung the administration of justice nationally as to provide a "field day" for criminal elements, including criminal hijackers.[7] To the extent that the major "airline" States themselves may have failed satisfactorily to strike the balance between interests in public safety and criminal due process, and that light national penalties for hijackers or laxness or carelessness in on-the-ground, pre-flight, screenings and searches of passengers and luggage may have facilitated or encouraged hijackers, the World Community is hardly responsible for having to fill the resultant gaps in an effective international air security system. The ultimate responsibility for these particular deficiencies falls upon the individual nation-States directly concerned; and it is significant that since the United States finally acted, in terms of the Presidential order of 5 December 1972, to institute an effective preventive control system at US airports to remedy the practical breakdown of attempts at collective, international control measures over hijacking, a reasonably fool-proof security system seems at last in process of emergence.[8] The World Community has affirmative obligations, to be sure, to coordinate and supplement and extend such national measures, by ensuring full and honest application of the *aut dedere, aut punire* principle in relation to hijackers; but it seems reasonably entitled to ask individual nation-States first to put their own houses in order and to reform or strengthen their own internal, anti-hijacking police control measures before complaining too loudly that the significant failure of community

---

The other day in Brooklyn a white social worker held out against 11 other jurors to prevent conviction in an airlines hijacking case. The black jury foreman said, 'I put my head in my hands and cried for an hour'." *Editorial,* "Getting Serious about Drugs", *The Wall Street Journal,* 23 January 1973.

7. "At Mr. Trapnell's first trial, which ended last January 15 . . ., the jury was split 11-to-1 for conviction for air piracy. Both the judge and fellow jurors bitterly criticised the lone holdout, Gertrude Haas, an unemployed psychiatric social worker who had worked for 30 years as a psychiatric therapist.

The retrial . . . opened on Monday before Chief Judge Jacob Mishler. After questioning the panel of prospective jurors about their occupations and their possible acquaintance with psychiatrists, he excused a social worker." *New York Times,* 9 May 1973.

8. The pre-flight boarding, preventive ground control screenings and searches of passengers and carry-on hand luggage, went into force—in terms of the US Presidential order of 5 December 1972—on 5 January 1973. In the first five months of the operation of this new *national* system of control in the United States, absolutely no cases of hijacking of aircraft were reported as occurring in the United States.

problem-solving, up-to-date, in regard to aerial hijacking, is all the fault of the World Community and its organised general and special political institutions like the UN Security Council and General Assembly and, not least, the International Civil Aviation Organisation.

POSTSCRIPT

AERIAL PIRACY AS INTERNATIONAL TERRORISM. THE DEVELOPMENT OF LEGAL CONTROLS

The conceived clogging or attrition of the normal constitutional-legal processes of community change, both within the traditional nation-state and also, more broadly, in the World Community, has brought with it a new emphasis upon extra-legal "direct action".

This is especially true of forms of direct action having a high public relations impact that, simply because they are spectacular, can expect instant and World-wide dissemination by the main mass communications media and presumably, in the process, cause some spill-off in terms of publicising of the aims and objectives of the activist groups involved. The recourse to the more spectacular forms of direct action has become more pronounced in recent times with the *embourgeoisement* of some of the more traditional revolutionary groups that, in the past, have been content with building upon a traditional dogmatic, doctrinal base and relying upon the slow processes of proselytising and political education to spread their message and convert the masses. It is, in fact, the successful penetration of the radical protest movements by socially-privileged, upper-*bourgeois* elements,—the "radical *chic*" —that has managed to make violence in claimed pursuit of revolutionary aims "radical *chic*" in itself.

It may be suggested that the "radical *chic*" element in the "new politics" sometimes seems rather fuzzy-minded as to what it is actually setting out to achieve, and, in particular, often seems to fail altogether to quantify the social costs of its action programmes, involving a balancing of the desired objectives (assuming that these have been coherently defined in the first place) against the expenditure of human energy and resources and the loss or gain of community good-will involved in their realisation. Applying objective, social scientific tests such as these to the direct action techniques of some contemporary radical protest movements, many of the measures resorted to seem to be quite counter-productive, if not down-right irrational. The English stock-broker millionaire's daughter with a Ph.D. degree who lectured at the

University of London and who stole priceless oil-paintings in Ireland, early in 1974, because she had some views, (never clearly communicated), on the Protestant-Catholic conflicts in Northern Ireland, may perhaps have demonstrated that the World's art treasures—as a common heritage of man-kind—should never be permitted to be stored in inadequately protected private homes; but any worthwhile contribution to solution of the "Irish problem" was surely negatived by the public outrage at her casual and careless treatment of the "old masters" while they were in her temporary possession, and by the evidence—suggesting past parent-child conflicts as the motivation for her acts—that she had previously stolen art treasures from her own father. The 35-year old wife of a well-known and wealthy Paris public relations director who, in October, 1973, hijacked an Air France Boeing-727 on a Paris-Nice flight and forced it to land at Marseilles, and was then killed in a shoot-out on the ground, apparently wanted to produce an Israeli-Arab reconciliation: the three page letter that she delivered to the aircraft's commander, in flight, was stated to be "so incoherent that, at the end of several lines, I didn't think it useful to finish reading it". In the same vein, though with rather less tragic results, in August, 1973, a young Arab, described as seeming to have drunk too many whiskies, successfully hijacked a Lebanese passenger aircraft on a flight from Libya to Beirut and forced it to land at Tel-Aviv, declaring that he "wanted to demonstrate that the Arab people did not hate the Jews". Patricia Hearst and the so-called Symbionese Liberation Army, it may be suggested, reveal a somewhat similar cloudiness as to ultimate purposes, and as to the relation, if any, between ends and means.

It is the counter-productive aspect of so many of these individual, isolated acts of terrorism which, on examination, seem to bear many of the characteristics of the "lunatic fringe" hijackings identified in the within lectures, that has caused the official, institutionalised and bureaucratised, guerilla organisations which, in certain cases, have taken on something of a quasi-governmental character, (with all the responsibilities of rational decision-making in pursuit of organisation objectives going with that quasi-public status), increasingly to dissociate themselves from fringe terrorist groups claiming the same objectives as themselves; and, in a number of cases, publicly to disown responsibility for particularly spectacular terrorist actions loosely attributed to them. Thus it was made known, after three Arab gunmen seized control of the Saudi Arabian Embassy in Paris in September, 1973, and took hostages whom they released only in return for safe conduct to an airport and embarkation and flight to a friendly Arab country, that the Palestine Liberation Organisation (PLO), the main, quasi-official Palestine guerrilla organisation, repudiated all responsibility for those individual terrorists whom it did not hesitate to characterise as "outlaws" and "renegades". Among other un-sanctioned acts of terrorism for which the Palestine Liberation Organisation also denied any responsibility were the July 19, 1973, attack by an armed Palestinian on the Israeli El Al Airline office in Athens, in which the lives of fifteen hostages were bargained for a safe passage to Kuwait; the hijacking of a Japan Air Lines Boeing-747, with 145 passengers aboard, from Amsterdam to Dubai, by a Japanese radical and a Latin American female guerrilla; and the August 5, 1973, shooting spree at the Athens International Airport, by an Egyptian and a Palestinian, in which three persons were killed and fifty-five wounded. In the case of the latter attack, the gunmen had intended to fire on passengers on a plane leaving for Tel-Aviv, but that plane had already taken-off ten minutes before, and the gunmen fired, in error, on passengers leaving on another plane for New York: on being told of their error the two gunmen burst out laughing. (*L'Express,* Paris, August 20, 1973).

Reference to the difficulties being experienced even by extra-constitutional political organisations like the Palestine Liberation Organisation, which are, by definition, themselves committed to use of extra-legal methods where judged necessary by them, in trying to control or prevent what they deem to be irrational, irresponsible, or down-right counter-productive terrorist actions by isolated individuals or splinter groups, indicates the problems in seeking to apply and make use of the international law doctrine of State Responsibility as a control for international terrorist activities. If an unofficial guerrilla organisation can experience such practical difficulties in controlling its own ideological kin, how much more of a problem may it be for an official, *de jure* government! The notion of international sanctions against a "delinquent" government failing effectively to deal with international terrorists operating within or from its borders may become harder politically to justify, at least in those cases where the government concerned is a purely involuntary host unable itself to control the terrorists and not actively aiding or harbouring them. Yet, the balance sheet of international terrorist activities shows that, failing an effective exercise of State Responsibility by individual Nation-States and in the absence of any international controls with teeth in them, the terrorists have so very much in their favour: according to a *New York Times* survey made at the beginning of 1974, of Arab terrorist acts against airline passengers or airline companies themselves since 1968, out of a total of 71 Arab terrorists actually apprehended for such acts of aerial piracy, only four were then currently serving a prison sentence. Of the remaining terrorists, four had been killed in the act, and the rest had either been rescued by other terrorists (normally by forced ransoming of innocent airline passengers taken hostage in further aircraft hijackings), or else released by their captors. Yet these aerial pirates' victims totalled 41 dead and 89 wounded.

The temptation to individual Nation-States that have been the especial targets or victims of international terrorist activities, to resort to direct action themselves in the absence of timely and energetic responses by other Nation-States that temporarily have custody of individual aerial pirates within their borders, and in the absence, equally, of effective international control machinery, may be great. On August 10, 1973, two Israeli Air Force fighters intercepted a Lebanese commercial passenger Caravelle on a flight from Baghdad to Beirut and forced it to land at Haifa, Israel. The Israeli intelligence agencies had had reason to believe that Dr. George Habbache, the founder of the Palestinian "Black September" terrorist group, the chief source of Arab assassins today, was aboard the aircraft; but Dr. Habbache had apparently decided not to board the aircraft in Baghdad because he had recognized the pilot as being a Jordanian national and he had vowed hatred and mistrust to the Jordanian Government. At the special reunion of the International Civil Aviation Organisation held in Rome in the late Summer of 1973, the Assembly of ICAO voted, on August 30, 1973, to condemn Israel for the forced diversion of the Lebanese aircraft, the censure being adopted by 87 votes to 1 (Israel), with 4 abstentions (Bolivia, Republic of Ireland, Singapore, and Thailand). Apparently, the very large vote against Israel was assisted by the fact that the Arab states decided, in concert with some African states—thus creating a bloc of 30 votes—not to insist on any sanctions against Israel for the action (*The Times,* (London), August 31, 1973); *Le Monde,* (Paris), September 1, 1973).

The special reunion of ICAO, held in Rome in the late Summer of 1973, had been convoked, it will be recalled, to consider concrete measures for international control of Aerial Piracy. But when the meetings were adjourned on September 20, 1973, after 25 days of debates and discussions, no agreement had been reached. The ICAO Assembly rejected, severally, the Soviet proposal for an additional protocol to The Hague Convention of 1970 (on the Suppression of Unlawful Seizure of Aircraft) providing for the compulsory extradition by each contracting state of hijackers coming into its territories in preference to trial by its own criminal authorities, (voted 47 countries *for,* 25 *against,* and 18 *abstentions,* and so failing because achieving less than a two-thirds majority); the Greek proposal concerning acts of terrorism committed in airports (voted 43 *for,* 28 *against,* and 20 *abstentions,* and thus short of a two-thirds majority); the French proposal for the inclusion in the Chicago Convention of 1944 itself of additional dispositions directed to the control of aerial piracy and which would have involved the expulsion from ICAO of delinquent states; and British-Swiss proposals that would have called on all countries to close their airspace to airlines of states refusing either to extradite or themselves to prosecute hijackers.

The apparent completeness of the failure of international action designed to achieve effective international control over aerial piracy, is tempered by success on other fronts. Impressive advance security and detection measures by the Italian police and intelligence services foiled altogether, on September 5, 1973, an elaborate plot staged by a group of five Arab terrorists (a Libyan, an Iraqi, a Jordanian, an Algerian, and a Lebanese) to shoot down civilian aircraft flying in or out of Rome's Fiumicino International Airport: the terrorists had intended to use two Soviet-built rocket launchers, firing ground-to-air missiles with a range of five kilometres, from a base in the Rome seaside resort of Ostia, next-door to the airport (*Corriere della Sera* (Milano), September 6, 1973). At the same time, official governmental statistics available up to the time of writing indicate that the last successful hijacking attempt on a civilian passenger aircraft in the United States occurred on November 10, 1972,—that is, immediately prior to President Nixon's executive decree instituting effective, on-the-ground, pre-flight, police inspection and control procedures at airports, and implementing certain other, related control measures. United States Senator Vance Hartke's last-ditch fight against the U.S. Federal Aviation Administration and such airport security measures on the argument that they violate the United States Constitution, at least when they are applied to members of Congress, has apparently received its quietus with the ruling by Federal District Judge Aubrey E. Robinson, jr., in Washington, D.C., on February 15, 1974, citing the United States Supreme Court in support of the proposition that—"legislators ought not to stand above the law they create but ought generally to be bound by it as are ordinary persons." (The *New York Times,* February 16, 1974). The House of Representatives in Washington, D.C., voted on March 13, 1974, (by 286 votes to 121), to apply the death penalty to airplane hijackers who cause death; and it also voted, at the same time, to overturn a court decision of February, 1974, banning airport security X-rays of passenger luggage at airports until such time as X-rays should be found safe; and finally it voted to codify existing security measures exercised by the Federal Aviation Administration, airlines, and airport operators (*The Wall Street Journal,* New York, March 14, 1974). Meanwhile, the various private, civil actions by airline passengers against airline companies, on the score of hijacking incidents, continue before the U.S. federal courts, albeit with "all deliberate speed". (See, in this regard, *American Journal of International Law,* vol. 66 at p. 870 (1972); *ibid.,* vol. 67 at 549 and 550 (1973); A. E. Evans, Aircraft Hijacking: What is being done? *ibid.,* vol. 67 at 641 (1973); O. J. Lissitzyn, In-Flight Crime and United States legislation, *ibid.,* vol. 67 at 306 (1973); *International Legal Materials* (American Society of International Law), vol. 12 (no. 6) at 1445 (November, 1973).)

What the record indicates is that, in default of any really concerted and energetic international control action, as to aerial piracy, that really has some teeth in it—a situation that we look like having to live with, in the present state of international relations, for some further, indefinite period of time—there are substantial, and probably perfectly ample, effective control measures available to individual governments and their national airlines if only they are prepared to be resolute and to court any risks of temporary political unpopularity involved in applying those measures to their own nationals and to foreign nationals choosing to use their airlines or their airports and airline installations. Contrary to some predictions, the American civilian airline passenger has adapted himself quickly and gracefully to the on-the-ground, pre-flight, inspection and control measures applied at airports against aerial piracy; there has been little or no adverse effect on airline time-tables; and the extra costs have been rather easily built in to existing airline operating costs or else assumed by the various governments (federal, state, municipal) concerned, without any undue economic burden being imposed thereby on either airline company or governmental budgets. The mystery may remain as to why it took so long for governments and airlines to act in these matters; and as to why some governments and airlines outside North America, Western Europe, and the Soviet bloc, still refuse to implement similar standards of excellence (combining maximum physical security for passengers with minimum inconvenience to passengers), this lack being evidenced by the still-continuing successful attacks on aircraft, airports and airline installations in various parts of the World.

In the area of international action, the total success of the United States-Cuban accords as to control of hijacking, both the earlier, informal arrangements and the later, formal agreement of 1972, is still further evidence, if any were now needed, that it is not always necessary to go after the universal, multilateral agreement, which, even when it is finally achieved, is too often, because of the need for achieving minimum consensus between too many ideologically disparate groups, bland and general to the point of being legally vacuous or meaningless. The scope for international problem-solving through the achievement of bilateral, or limited number, accords between two or more parties that, whatever their general political-ideological differences, have a common consensus on pragmatic, empirical solutions for concrete and immediate problems common to each of them, is considerable; and such bilateral or limited accords can then serve as models, if need be, for a further range of bilateral or limited accords with other countries, thereby giving rise to more general or overarching principles through a series of interlocking, limited agreements. Rather than have us wait indefinitely for the "Sermon on the Mount" in the form of yet another near-universal, multilateral treaty involving some further statement of abstract general principles as to the control of aerial piracy, all the evidence suggests that the main airline states within the "special legal community" of the air should proceed to maximise their own special power base by looking to development of their own control measures adapted to their own specific needs, and by increasingly coordinating and harmonising those measures with one another.

ADDENDUM 1

AERIAL PIRACY. QUESTIONS FOR DISCUSSION

1. To what extent, if at all, is the problem of aerial hijacking covered by existing international (customary) law, including (though not limited to) the customary international law as to piracy?

2. What are the advantages and limitations of the *multinational,* multilateral convention-based approach to international legal problem-solving in this area as illustrated by the success or otherwise of the Tokyo Convention of 1963 and later multilateral conventions in the field of aerial hijacking?

3. What are the relative merits of the *national* (as opposed to multinational) approach to the solution of aerial hijacking problems, including the national negotiation of bilateral (or limited, regional) accords concerning control; unilateral national administrative action within the framework of, or not incompatible with, existing international air law accords: national legislation; national police control action, including airport surveillance and screenings?

4. What are the relative merits of *private,* as opposed to *public* (inter-governmental or governmental) action or initiatives,—for example, action by the Airline Pilots' Associations: Airport trade unions; individual private legal actions (in contract, delict)?

5. Assuming successful adoption and application of the multilateral convention-based approach, involving *inter alia* compulsory application of criminal extradition procedures to aerial hijackers, what *rôle,* if any, should be accorded to the so-called "political exception" in favour of *bona fide* requests for political asylum? In other words, should the right to request, and the right of a State to grant, political asylum be any different as between hijackers and other species of delinquents? If not, what legal differentations or conditions would you establish as to claims to political asylum as a human right advanced by, or in behalf of, hijackers?

6. Should one favor the principle of hue and cry as to criminal jurisdiction over hijackers,—meaning here, if not universality, at least multiple or plural jurisdiction, with all states having some minimal contact with a particular problem-situation having criminal jurisdiction? What should be the attitude towards the idea of international

jurisdiction, including possibly jurisdiction of an international tribunal?

7. What balance should be made between the principle of the "freedom of air" and other, possibly countervailing, legal values sometimes asserted in aerial hijacking problem-situations,—for example, the principle of national self-determination? In other words, may aerial hijacking conceivably sometimes be licit, in international law terms, as a means of effectuating national policies, or even group or individual policies? If so, what might be other international law principles conditioning the effective legal vindication of such a claim, in such circumstances?

8. What convergence or divergence of basic interests and policies can be found as between the different members of the international "special legal community" involved in the aerial hijacking problem-area, for example, international inter-governmental organizations (the U.N.; ICAO); international private associations (IATA; IFALPA); national governments; private individuals (passengers)? What effects do these differences—including, for example, even within the one interest-group, national governments, differences between the Big Powers and the small states—have upon the choice of policies (objectives) and also strategies (instruments) for control of aerial hijacking, and even upon the time-table for control?

9. To what extent does the problem of aerial hijacking lend itself to some one general or comprehensive or universal solution rather than to a number of necessarily more limited and particularised solutions?

10. As an operational question, what particular aspects of the aerial hijacking problem-situation should be seen as most immediately promising or "ripe" in terms of solution and therefore as deserving of priority in terms of community problem-solving attempts; and what aspects, by contrast, can be regarded as unlikely to yield concrete solutions at this time? What operational strategies (including recommendations for specific machinery-institutional approaches) may be advanced for application to the "priority" aspects so favored?

ADDENDUM 2

SELECTED BIBLIOGRAPHY

Aerial Piracy and International Law, Edward McWhinney (Editor) (1971) (A. W. Sijthoff, Leiden; Oceana Publications, New York):
p. 15, Edward McWhinney; "International Legal Problem-Solving and the practical dilemma of Hijacking".
— p. 27, Charles F. Butler; "The path to International Legislation against Hijacking".
— p. 55, Michel Pourcelet; "Comment: Hijacking. The Limitations of the International Treaty Approach".
— p. 59, John B. Rhinelander; "The International Law of Aerial Piracy. New Proposals for the New Dimension".
— p. 97, Haroldo Valladão; "Punition internationale de l'actuelle piraterie aérienne".
— p. 116, Oliver J. Lissitzyn; "Hijacking, International Law, and Human Rights".
p. 124, L. C. Green; "Hijacking and the Right of Asylum".

Institut de droit international, Annuaire, Vol. 54, Session of Zagreb (August-September 1971);
— Tome 1, pp. 520-669 (Eighteenth Commission, Hijacking of Aircraft, *Provisional Report*) (Edward McWhinney, rapporteur).
— Tome 1, pp. 670-769 (Eighteenth Commission, Hijacking of Aircraft, *Final Report*) (Edward McWhinney, rapporteur).
— Tome 2, pp. 346-403, séance plénière. "Le détournement illicite des aéronefs".
— Tome 2, pp. 455-458, 471-474, "Résolutions. Le détournement illicite des aéronefs".

New Developments in the Law of International Aviation: The Control of Aerial Hijacking. (Symposium; *Proceedings of American Society of International Law,* Sixty-fifth Annual Meeting, 1971), pp. 71-96:
— p. 71, Edward McWhinney (Chairman/président);
— p. 75, K. E. Malmborg, Jr.;
— p. 80, Oliver J. Lissitzyn;
— p. 86, Andreas F. Lowenfeld;
— p. 89, Alona E. Evans.

Alex Meyer, *Luftpiraterie. Begriff, Tatbestände, Bekämpfung,* 1972.

P. de La Pradelle, "L'enlèvement aérien des chefs fellagah", *Revue générale de l'air* (Vol. 19, 1956), p. 235.

M. E. Valay, "Le déroutement des aéronefs", *Revue générale de l'air et de l'espace* (Vol. 32, 1969), p. 340.

P. de La Pradelle, "Les détournements d'aéronefs et le droit international", *Revue générale de l'air et de l'espace* (Vol. 32, 1969), p. 249.

Charles Rousseau, "Détournement et destruction par des commandos palestiniens de quatre avions commerciaux—deux américains, un suisse et un britannique (6 et 9 septembre 1970)", *Revue générale de droit international public* (1970, Vol. 4), p. 1018.

Charles Rousseau, "Algérie et Congo-Kinshasa: enlèvement en avion de M. Moïse Tschombé au-dessus des Baléares et détention de l'ancien chef du Gouvernement congolais par les autorités algériennes (30 juin 1967), *Revue générale de droit international public* (1968, No. 1), p. 145.

Alex Meyer, "Luftpiraterie als Rechtsproblem", *Zeitschrift für Luftrecht und Weltraumrechtsfragen* (1969), p. 77.
Alex Meyer, "Un nouveau problème juridique: La piraterie aérienne", *Revue française de droit aérien* (1969), p. 261.
Alex Meyer, "Versicherungs- und Haftungsfragen bei Luftpiraterie", *Zeitschrift für Luftrecht und Weltraumrechtsfragen* (1970), p. 293.
E. du Pontavice, "La piraterie aérienne: notion et effets", *Revue générale de l'air et de l'espace* (Vol. 32, 1969), p. 276.
H. F. van Panhuys, "Aircraft Hijacking and International Law", *Columbia Journal of Transnational Law* (Vol. 9, 1970), p. 1.
J. W. F. Sundberg, "La piraterie aérienne. Petite étude sur la relation entre politique nationale et criminalité à l'étranger", *Revue internationale de droit pénal* (1970), p. 165.
M. Pourcelet, "La capture illicite d'aéronefs (Hijacking)", *Revue générale de l'air et de l'espace* (1969), p. 269.
Juglart, "Les infractions commises à bord des aéronefs dans la doctrine internationale", *Revue française de droit aérien* (1960), p. 123, p. 227.
R. H. Mankiewicz, "Capture et détournements illicites d'aéronefs", *Annuaire français de droit international* (Vol. 15, 1969), p. 462.
R. H. Mankiewicz, "Le détournement d'avions", *Revue française de droit aérien* (1971), p. 392.
S. Glasser, "Quelques observations sur le détournement d'aéronefs", *Revue générale de droit international public* (Vol. 76, 1972), p. 12.
A. E. Evans, "Aircraft Hijacking: Its Cause and Cure", *American Journal of International Law* (Vol. 63, 1969), p. 695.
A. E. Evans, "Aircraft Hijacking: What is to be done?", *American Journal of International Law* (Vol. 66, 1972), p. 819.
Ya. Makhovskii, "Zakhvat grazhdanskogo vosdushnogo sudna v svete mezhdunarodnogo prava", *Sovetskoe Gosudarstvo i Pravo* (1971, No. 8), p. 59.
P. Yevseyev, Yu. Kolosov, "Air Bandits Outlawed", *International Affairs* (Moscow) (1971, No. 8), p. 83.
W. Abendroth, "Piraterie", H. J. Schlochauer (Editor), *Wörterbuch des Völkerrechts* (Vol. 2, 1961), p. 768.
V. V. Pella, "La répression des crimes contre la personnalité de l'Etat", *Recueil des cours de l'Académie de droit international de La Haye* (1930), III, p. 677.
A. Sottile, "Le Terrorisme International", *Recueil des cours de l'Académie de Droit international de La Haye* (1938), III, p. 91.
C. Eustathiades, "La cour pénale internationale pour la répression du terrorisme et le problème de la responsabilité internationale des Etats", *Revue générale de droit international public* (Vol. 43, 1936), p. 385.
H. Donnedieu de Vabres, "La répression internationale du terrorisme. Les Conventions de Genève (16 novembre 1937)", *Revue de droit international et de législation comparée* (3rd Series, Vol. 19, 1938), p. 37.
von Gretshaninow, "Der Plan eines internationalen Abkommen betreffend die Bekämpfung politischen Verbrechen und die Errichtung eines internationalen Strafgerichtshof", *Zeitschrift für ausländisches öffentliches Recht und Völkerrecht* (Vol. 5, 1935), p. 181.
H. Mosler, "Die Konferenz zur internationalen Bekämpfung des Terrorismus (November 1937)", *Zeitschrift für ausländisches öffentliches Recht und Völkerrecht* (Vol. 8, 1938), p. 99.
Corfu Channel Case (Merits), *International Court of Justice*, 1949, *Reports of Judgments,* Judgment of 9 April 1949.

H. Krüger, "Seenot" (H. J. Schlochauer, Editor), *Wörterbuch des Völkerrechts* (Vol. 3, 1962), p. 237.
N. M. Matte, *Traité de droit aérien-aéronautique* (2nd ed., 1964).
C. J. Colombos, *The International Law of the Sea* (4th revised edition, 1959).
Institut de droit international, *Annuaire* (Vol. 17, 1898), p. 284.
Institut de droit international, *Annuaire* (Vol. 34, 1928), p. 737.
International Law Association. Report of the Fifty-Fourth Conference (1971), *Committee on Piracy* (*Sea and Air*):
Introduction by D. H. N. Johnson, at p. 730.
Report by Haroldo Valladão, at p. 735.
Report by J. Sundberg, at p. 755.
American Journal of International Law, vol. 66, (1972), at p. 870;
Ibid., vol. 67 (1973), at pp. 549 & 550;
Ibid., vol. 68 (1974), p. 119 and p. 531.
International Legal Materials (American Society of International Law), (vol. 12, 1973), p. 1445.
S. K. Agrawala, *Aircraft Hijacking and International Law* (1973).
Aktualnie voprosii mezhdunarodnogo vozdushnogo prava (1973).
C. Emanuelli, Etude des moyens de prévention et de sanction en cas d'action illicite contre l'aviation civile internationale, *Revue Générale de Droit International Public;* vol. 77 (1973) p. 577.
A. E. Evans, Aircraft Hijacking: What is being done?, *American Journal of International Law;* vol. 67, (1973), p. 641.
E. W. Faller, *Gewaltsame Flugzeugentführungen aus völkerrechtlicher Sicht* (1972).
G. F. FitzGerald, Concerted action against States found in default of their international obligations in respect of unlawful interference with International Civil Aviation, *Canadian Yearbook of International Law,* vol. 10, (1972), p. 261.
K. Hailbronner, Entführte Flugzeuge auf fremden Staatsgebiet und die analoge Anwendung humanitärer Grundsätze im Völkerrecht, *Zeitschrift für ausländisches öffentliches Recht und Völkerrecht,* vol. 32, (1972), p. 265.
Y. Kolosov, Legal questions of the security of Civil Aviation, *International Affairs* (Moscow), (1974) no. 4, p. 42.
O. J. Lissitzyn, In-Flight Crime and United States Legislation, *American Journal of International Law*, vol. 67, (1973), p. 306.